REST IS RESISTANCE

REST IS RESISTANCE

A MANIFESTO

TRICIA HERSEY

Little, Brown Spark
New York Boston London

Little, Brown Spark
Hachette Book Group
1290 Avenue of the Americas, New York, NY 10104
littlebrownspark.com

First Edition: October 2022

Little, Brown Spark is an imprint of Little, Brown and Company, a division of Hachette Book Group, Inc. The Little, Brown Spark name and logo are trademarks of Hachette Book Group, Inc.

Library of Congress Control Number: 2022942591

Printing 5, 2023

ISBN 9780316365215

LSC-C

Printed in the United States of America

The book is dedicated to my daddy, Elder Willie James Hersey.
When I was child and wanted to travel to the moon,
thank you for buying me luggage from Sears department store.
You are my greatest Ancestor.

CONTENTS

Preface 3

Introduction 9

Part One: **REST!** 43

Part Two: **DREAM!** 91

Part Three: **RESIST!** 127

Part Four: **IMAGINE!** 157

Acknowledgments 197

The Nap Ministry Library 199

Notes 201

Index 203

Your body is a site of liberation.
It doesn't belong to capitalism.
Love your body.
Rest your body.
Move your body.
Hold your body.

I hope you are reading this while laying down!

REST IS RESISTANCE

PREFACE

Rest saved my life. This is my truth. I don't need anyone else to verify this nor do I need complicated theories to support what I know to be true in my heart, my body, and my Spirit. My pilgrimage with rest as a form of resistance and liberation practice is a deeply personal one. It is one that started way before anyone heard of The Nap Ministry on social media. Resting was my attempt to solve a problem in my life and like most Black women before me, I worked within the realms of my own life and history to create a way.

While in a brutally busy graduate program, with financial issues, family illness, and the threat of racial violence always swirling around, I started to experiment with rest. My commitment to rest as a form of resistance came from my everyday experiences of being a part of the machine-level pace of our culture and surviving the trauma of the terror of poverty, exhaustion, white supremacy, and capitalism. I took to napping all over campus while in seminary and when I was home. I believed deeply that I would rest because I was exhausted physically and spiritually, and I saw no other way to make it. I was beyond rational thought about whether I would be able to thrive from this and simply leaped without a net.

I was fueled by the deep history of cultural trauma I was studying while in seminary. I was reading slave narratives while studying Jim Crow terrorism and falling asleep with the book on my chest. I was guided by Harriet Tubman, proclaiming after waking up from a prophetic dream: "My people are free." The audacity to proclaim freedom via rest in the now. Rest has been revolutionary for my soul.

This book is a testimony and testament of my refusal to donate my body to a system that still owes a debt to my Ancestors for the theft of their labor and DreamSpace. I refuse to push my body to the brink of exhaustion and destruction. Let the chips fall where they may. I trust myself more than capitalism. Our refusal will make space for abundance. We will have to leap and trust rest. May the ground underneath hold us, and if we must collapse, may a soft pillow be there. This book is a scream on a bullhorn for the collective to join me in disrupting and pushing back. The Nap Ministry is a warm blanket swaddling us all back to our deepest selves. A more human place. A resting place.

It is never easy to explain why I started The Nap Ministry. It is so layered, nuanced, and organic. I have been asked the question of its origin thousands of times by strangers, journalists, and social media followers. Everyone is thirsty for the quick details of why I would dream up a project about napping. I am elated the story has not been an easy and direct answer, because like decolonizing, it will take enormous effort in the form of radical healing, change, redemption, and collective care.

Everything always starts with the personal. The origins of The Nap Ministry begin with the story of my family in fragmented parts. The microhistories and small details of our lives hold the keys to our redemption. My rest resurrection begins with my desperation to find relief from my own exhaustion via curiosity, experimentation, and self-preservation.

I come from a legacy of exhaustion. My maternal grandmother, Ora, the muse of this work, a refugee from Jim Crow terrorism, rested her eyes every day for thirty minutes to an hour in an attempt to connect and find peace. My great-grandmother Rhodie, I am told, stayed up late nightly on her farm in deep Mississippi with a pistol in her apron pocket to creatively solve any problems from the Ku Klux Klan. The reality of our survival from white supremacy and capitalism is deeply shocking to me. I am in awe at what our bodies can hold. We must lighten our loads. Survival is not the end goal for liberation. We must thrive. We must rest.

As a child, I would watch my grandmother Ora as she sat on her plastic-covered yellow couch and meditated for thirty minutes every single day. She fled her home in Mississippi with thousands of other African-Americans during the Great Migration of the 1950s. Ora floated up North on a spaceship built from uncertainty and hope as she landed in Chicago. She magically raised eight children, while dodging poverty, racism, and the invisibility of being a Black woman in America. Her commitment to "resting her eyes" every day for thirty minutes was radical. Her ability to demand space to "just be" was a form of resistance.

While my grandmother rested her eyes, I would tiptoe around her home trying not to wake her up. I always thought she was sleeping while sitting up. I was curious about her rest practice and thought she was so eccentric. Whenever I would inquire if she was sleeping, her response was always the same: "Every shut eye ain't sleep. I am resting my eyes and listening for what God wants to tell me." While all the world around her was attempting to crush her Spirit, she rested and resisted the beast of grind culture. She taught my mother to rest, she taught me to rest. I am humbled to be a vessel to guide thousands on their own rest journey as we embrace rest as a way to make us all more human.

My inspiration to rest is deep and expansive. I'm inspired by invention and the opportunity to craft something new from scratch. I'm inspired by remixing and being subversive. I am inspired by disruption and tenderness. I am inspired by imagination. I am inspired by grief, mourning, and lament. I believe deeply in vulnerable, generative spaces for healing. I am inspired by rest, daydreaming, and sleep.

Our collective rest will not be easy. All of culture is collaborating for us not to rest. I understand this deeply. We are sleep-deprived because the systems view us as machines, but bodies are not machines. Our bodies are a site of liberation. We are divine and our rest is divine. There is synergy, interconnectedness, and deep communal healing within our rest movement. I believe rest, sleep, naps, daydreaming, and slowing down can help us all wake up to see the truth of ourselves. Rest is a healing portal to our deepest selves. Rest is care. Rest is radical.

We must stand and lay firmly in the space of creating a life filled with rest and radical care, even amid oppression. Rest Is Resistance is our tagline and mantra. Our call. Rest is a form of resistance because it disrupts and pushes back against capitalism and white supremacy. Both these toxic systems refuse to see the inherent divinity in human beings and have used bodies as a tool for production, evil, and destruction for centuries. Grind culture has made us all human machines, willing and ready to donate our lives to a capitalist system that thrives by placing profits over people. The Rest Is Resistance movement is a connection and a path back to our true nature. We are stripped down to who we really were before the terror of capitalism and white supremacy. We are enough. We are divine.

If we are not resting, we will not make it. I need us to make it. We must thrive. I know our collective rest will liberate us and shift consciousness. A rest movement. A spiritual movement. A political movement rooted in care and justice. The deprogramming from our brainwashing will take intention and time. Rest is a meticulous love practice, and we will be unraveling from our sleep deprivation and socialization around rest for the remainder of our days. This is a blessing. Rest is radical because it disrupts the lie that we are not doing enough. It shouts: "No, that is a lie. I am enough. I am worthy now and always because I am here." The Rest Is Resistance movement is a connection and a path back to our true nature. We are stripped down to who we really were before the terror of capitalism and white supremacy. We are enough. We are divine. Our bodies don't belong to these toxic systems. We know better. Our Spirits know better.

The legacy of exhaustion stops with me. I invite you into the portal rest provides. Capitalism cannot have me. White supremacy cannot have me. Join me in reclaiming our DreamSpace. The time to rest is now.

INTRODUCTION

I wish you rest today. I wish you a deep knowing that exhaustion is not a normal way of living. You are enough. You can rest. You must resist anything that doesn't center your divinity as a human being. You are worthy of care.

I want this book to be a prayer. A field guide for the rest resistance. A document to be engaged with on the ground as we all navigate the reality of capitalism and white supremacy robbing us of our bodies, our leisure, and our DreamSpace. A blessing whispered over your body and around your head. An embodied pilgrimage toward rest. Let this be a testimony to our collective survival and our present and future thriving. You don't belong on the grind. Get off the violent cycle. It is burning down because we torched it. Grind culture can't have you.

Imagine a world without oppression.
Take more time here. Visualize softness.
Breathe deep.
Envision a world centered in justice.
Stay here.

Welcome to your DreamSpace. A download. A daydream. Stay here. Stay in rest. Stay in the DreamSpace. Our collective rest will save us. You are enough. Our dreams are enough. This is imagination work. A portal opens when we slow down. You can rest.

I'm dreaming of a world that includes justice for all those

sleep-deprived, exhausted, and caught up in the hustle and shenanigans of white supremacy and capitalism. May we have space to navigate our lives from a liberated rest state. May all of culture slow down. May we rest together.

I believe our entire culture is sleep-deprived and exhausted. So, if you are holding this book, I'm rejoicing because this book hopes to be a battle cry, a guidebook, a field guide, a pillow, and a map for the Rest Is Resistance movement. A manifesto for the weary and hopeful. An imagination tool.

People are waking up. People are waking up. People are waking up to the truth of their manipulation under toxic systems. People are waking up to heal. People are waking up to rest. We will no longer be a martyr for grind culture. Grind culture is a collaboration between white supremacy and capitalism. It views our divine bodies as machines. Our worth is not connected to how much we produce. Another way is possible. Our shared history is one of extreme disconnection and denial. We ignore our bodies' need to rest and in doing so, we lose touch with Spirit. In our bodies we have our temples. It is the only thing we own. Our bodies are a tool agent for change. A site of liberation. Our bodies know. The time to rest is now. Our collective rest will change the world because our rest resides in a Spirit of refusal and disruption. Rest is our protest. Rest is resistance. Rest is reparations.

I remain grateful for the mystery of the unknown, experimentation, and the constant demand for liberation no matter what the systems have told us. Grateful for our divinity that we can tap into no matter what we are living through. Grateful for the metaphysical, the telepathic, and the deep knowing that our worth is not connected to how much labor we can withstand. This rest message is a message of power over oppression. Rest is a balm. We Will Rest!

TENETS OF THE NAP MINISTRY

1. Rest is a form of resistance because it disrupts and pushes back against capitalism and white supremacy.
2. Our bodies are a site of liberation.
3. Naps provide a portal to imagine, invent, and heal.
4. Our DreamSpace has been stolen and we want it back. We will reclaim it via rest.

The above tenets came to me in a dream over the course of a few months when I began to search for ease by resting. Each one revealed and unlocked massive healing in my own consciousness and a profound connection to the ways grind culture weakens our love of self and community. When I wrote these tenets onto paper for the first time, I scribbled them into a composition notebook to ground my personal rest experimentation. I wanted to meditate on each one to make sense of what was happening in my Spirit as I reclaimed my time from the powers that be.

Tenet 1: Rest is a form of resistance because it disrupts and pushes back against capitalism and white supremacy.

The first tenet became a soft bell in my ear. It became my secret battle cry as I took to my bed or my couch to deepen into my connection with my Ancestors, to rest for them, to save my own life. Each time I arose from a rest moment, things felt different. I looked different, my thinking was different, things that I couldn't work out while awake made sense after a nap. I had a dream that included my grandmother Ora holding my hand and walking through a field of grass, the sun shining bright on our faces. We didn't walk for long and suddenly she was gesturing for me to make the field my bed. As I released her hand I slowly laid in the grass, and she laid right next to me. We were laying face-to-face, staring at each other intently. She was tracing my entire face with her eyes, and I was doing the same. The feeling of awe and wonder filled me, and I felt so safe, warm, and protected. I woke up from the dream with the widest smile. I didn't want it to end.

The systems have manipulated and socialized us so that we stay exhausted. We can remain stuck in a never-ending cycle of trauma. If we are not tapped into the truth of our divinity, there is the possibility of continued brainwashing. I have been asked thousands of times, "How do I rest and work so I can make a living?" or "I would love to rest more but I have bills. How is it possible?" I have been presented with the desperate question by so many exhausted people and it speaks to the crisis we are in as a culture.

Capitalism was created on plantations. The roots of it are violence and theft. We as a culture gloss over this historical truth. But, to dive into the cracks of this reality is where a profound part of your deprogramming from grind culture resides. To understand and meditate on this truth may place us all in a space of grief. We must grieve. Rest supports our grieving by allowing space, and with space we can begin healing from the trauma of grind culture. Grieving is a sacred act and one of the ways we can begin to reconnect with our bodies, as we craft a rest practice.

Capitalism has cornered us in such a way that we only can comprehend two options. 1: Work at a machine level, from a disconnected and exhausted place, or 2: Make space for rest and space to connect with our highest selves while fearing how we will eat and live. This rigid binary, combined with the violent reality of poverty, keeps us in a place of sleep deprivation and constant hustling to survive.

The work of liberation from these lies resides in our deprogramming and tapping into the power of rest and in our ability to be flexible and subversive. There are more than two options. The possibilities are infinite, although living under a capitalist system is to be confronted with a model of scarcity. This space makes you falsely believe there is not enough of everything: not enough money, not enough care, not enough love, not enough attention, not enough peace, not enough connection, not enough time. There is abundance.

The desperate and valid question of "How can I rest, if I have to pay bills?" is the beating heart of this work. It is evidence of the trauma endured by the hands of grind culture and evidence of our need to reimagine rest. Resting as a form of resistance will be part of a lifelong unraveling. A mind shift, a slow and consistent practice filled with grace. We must imagine a new way, and rest is the foundation for this invention. We should use every tool we have to constantly repair what grind culture has done to us. We will be disrupting and pushing back against grind culture for a lifetime. This fact should give us hope for the possibilities of a new future. Be inspired and hold the vision of rest close. We must collectively push back against any system that continues to disregard our divinity. To be colonized is to accept and buy into the lie of our worth being connected to how much we get done. Keep repeating to yourself: *I am enough now.* There is no way around this. We have all participated willingly and unwillingly in the allure of grind culture. We have done this because since birth, we slowly are indoctrinated into the cult of urgency and disconnection via white supremacy culture.

All of culture is working in collaboration for us not to rest, and when we do listen to our bodies and take rest, many feel extreme guilt and shame. Embrace knowing that you have been manipulated and scammed by a violent system as powerful evidence. Now with this knowledge you can grieve, repair, rest, and heal. We can rejoice for the beauty of a veil being removed. This is the beginning of the new world we can create. So, stay here in rest, even for a few minutes each day before leaping into the comfort of intellectualizing this rest work. Resting is an embodied practice and a lifelong unraveling. It is not something that can be trendy, quick, or shallow. Resting is ancient, slow, and connected work that will take hold of you in ways that may be surprising. Let deprogramming from grind culture surprise you. Let your entire being slowly begin to shift. Get lost in rest. Pull up the blankets, search for softness and be open to the ways rest will surprise and calm you.

I could tell ten thousand stories about moments when I have been filled with exhaustion. So many moments of watching my parents exhausted, my grandparents exhausted. Ten thousand stories and examples of moments where my body was pushed to the brink of true damage and true disconnection. I could share with you these tender quiet moments of me unaware if I could go on because my body and mind were so weary, tired, and pushed to the brink of pure exhaustion. I feel like a legacy of exhaustion resides somewhere in all of us, but specifically resides in the bodies of those who have melanated skin. To those who are descendants of plantation labor and those marginalized, this exhaustion is deep. Sleep deprivation is a public health issue and a spiritual issue. It is a spiritual issue for a few reasons. We have been trained to believe that everything we accomplish is because of our own pushing alone. This is false because there is a spiritual dimension that exists in all things and in everything we do. To understand that we are spiritual beings navigating life in a material world opens us to the possibilities of rest as a spiritual practice. Our entire living is a spiritual practice. Much of our resistance to rest, sleep, and slowing down is an ego problem. You believe you can and must do it all because of our obsession with individualism and our disconnection to spirituality. Nothing we accomplish in life is totally free of the influence of spirit and community. We do nothing alone.

I am clearly stating that to center rest, naps, sleep, slowing down, and leisure in a capitalist, white supremacist, ableist, patriarchal world is to live as an outlier. A pilgrimage infused with softness, intentionality, and community care. We will not be able to interrupt the machine of grind culture alone. We need each other in more ways than we are allowed to believe. This work is about radical community care.

Tenet 2: Our bodies are a site of liberation.

For us to be more human, returning to our natural state before the lies, terror, and trauma of this system. To be who we were before the terror of white supremacy, capitalism, and patriarchy is the power of resting. To no longer be ravaged by this culture's incessant need to keep going no matter what to produce at all costs. This is why we rest.

Grieving the reality of being manipulated to believe we are not enough, divine, or valuable outside of our accomplishments and bank account is a central part of our rest work. It is sad and disturbing. I only started to confront and acknowledge the grief present in me and so many others in 2015, when the foundation for The Nap Ministry really began to take shape. I understand that many reading this book have never sat with the grief and pain associated with attaching your worth to productivity and money. This fact alone is enough reason to rest. But you cannot simply just tell someone who has been traumatized by capitalism since birth to consistently lay down and rest without addressing the reality of our brainwashing. When we finally wake up to the truth of what a machine-level pace of labor has done to our physical bodies, our self-esteem, and our Spirits, the unraveling begins.

As I have counseled people who have an extreme desire to slow down and rest, I have witnessed the subtle and bold ways grind culture has swallowed us whole. Being a parent has opened my eyes up to the ways grind culture successfully begins its socialization of fear and urgency. Even before my son was born the medical industry was rushing him out of my womb. During my pregnancy, the doctor was obsessed with how large my son might possibly be. In my eighth month, their concern sent me to a specialist to receive an intensive ultrasound to rule out twins. I already knew I wasn't having twins and correctly predicted his gender. I knew he might be a larger baby because I am six feet tall and my entire family, including both parents, were over six feet tall. All the women in my family had larger babies. I shared this history with my doctor, but like many in the medical system, she didn't listen. On my last appointment, four days before his due date, she signaled that I would have to have a C-section because she was unsure I could deliver such a large baby. She also shared that the last larger baby she delivered had complications that she is now fighting in court because a lawsuit was filed. In her words, "Let's just get him out now."

I was mortified and pleaded with her to let me try and labor. I told her that he would not be nine or ten pounds like the scans showed. I responded with a deep confidence, "He will be eight pounds. I know this in my Spirit!" In a rushed and urgent tone, she said no, and I would be delivering that evening via C-section. I was crushed and went home crying as I prepared to make my way to the hospital to give birth. Once there, I had a successful C-section and when they put him on the scale he weighed eight pounds and zero ounces, exactly as I had predicted. The doctor was shocked and kept repeating, "You knew!"

What struck me about this experience is the deep ways in which capitalism was given full power to control and drive my son's entrance into the world. Grind culture has taken over every facet of our lives. The real fear of what could happen if we step into the unknown is crafted by capitalism and its cult of busyness and productivity. We are wrapped up in a web that feels inescapable and hopeless. Will you trust me and trust your divinity enough to believe it is indeed not hopeless? Can you trust, even for a second, that we can reside in a rested future? I ask for us to walk this road slowly together, lay down together and collectively care for each other in a way that makes rest possible.

Fear, which is a function of grind culture, was able to drive the doctor's thinking, leaving my intuition ignored and the pain and disappointment of an unnecessary cesarean section. The doctor wanted my son out immediately so that she could move on to her next patient without a lawsuit and the extended time of allowing the labor process to begin naturally.

Later, my son left the comfort of our slow-paced home into the public school system, and I began to watch slowly how his voice, connection to his body, and intuition were attacked. In elementary school, students are being trained to be workers who can follow orders, memorize facts, and be on time no matter what. Imagination and critical thinking skills are replaced with cookie-cutter learning and standardized testing. I would volunteer in my son's third grade classroom weekly and noticed the young children being told, "Hold your pee. Bathroom break isn't for another twenty minutes." I watched in horror as an eight-year-old squirmed, attempting to wait the twenty minutes until he could allow his body to relieve itself. The teacher, obviously overwhelmed with a large classroom, continued to ignore his cues and he eventually used the bathroom on himself. I helped to take him to the bathroom to clean up and walked him to the office so his parents could be called to bring a change of clothes.

This blatant disregard of his body and the unnecessary embarrassment he and other students suffer in public school systems begin the process of learning to ignore the needs of your body. The brainwashing starts. The removal of physical education, recess, and nap time from public schools is more evidence of a culture unconcerned with space, connection, and slowing down. This ongoing socialization and manipulation by the systems then become internalized and we become the agents of grind culture.

Many people believe grind culture is this pie-in-the-sky monster directing our every move, when in reality, we become grind culture. We are grind culture. Grind culture is our everyday behaviors, expectations, and engagements with each other and the world around us. We have been socialized, manipulated, and indoctrinated by everything in culture to believe the lies of grind culture. In order for a capitalist system to thrive, our false beliefs in productivity and labor must remain. We have internalized its teachings and become zombie-like in Spirit and exhausted in body. So we push ourselves and each other under the guise of being hyperproductive and efficient. From a very young age we begin the slow process of disconnecting from our bodies' need to rest and are praised when we work ourselves to exhaustion. We tell our children to "stop being lazy" when they aren't participating in work culture with the same intensity as us. We lose empathy for ourselves first and push excessively. We become managers, teachers, and leaders who fall prey to the allure of a capitalist system and treat those we have the honor of working with as human machines. We become rigid and impatient when our checklist isn't completed to perfection. We become less human and less secure. We believe we are only meant to survive and not thrive. We see care as unnecessary and unimportant. We believe we don't really have to rest. We falsely believe hard work guarantees success in a capitalist system. I have been told this constantly for as long as I can remember. On nights when I worked two jobs, still unable to pay my bills on time or save, I continued to tell myself, "Burn the midnight oil, keep working hard, go to college, find a third job and a side hustle." I clearly remember the moment it clicked for me how a capitalist, patriarchal, ableist, anti-Black system could never make space for the success I wanted for myself. The "success" grind culture props up centers constant labor, material wealth, and overworking as a badge of honor. Resting is about the beginning process of undoing trauma so that we can thrive and evolve back to our natural state: a state of ease and rest.

We are meant to survive, and ultimately thrive, because we are divine. All of culture is in collaboration for us not to rest. This includes: K–12 public education, higher education, faith and religious denominations, medical industry and not-for-profits, activist organizations, corporations. Even those who claim to be a part of the wellness industry are pushing hustling, grinding, capitalism, girl boss, competition, and co-opting the work of Indigenous practices for clout and money. I believe academia is the headquarters for grind culture, and it is a full-circle moment that the energy and idea for The Nap Ministry came to me while I was suffering from exhaustion in a graduate school program.

Our everyday behaviors and false beliefs about productivity drive us into behaving in a robotic, machine-like way. The way we hold ourselves and others to the lie of urgency is white supremacy culture and we will never be able to rest or be liberated from oppression while we are honoring and aligning with it. Liberation and oppression cannot occupy the same space. It's not possible. We must go slow and place intention at the forefront of this disruption. This work is not simply a reminder to rest, but a full interruption and turning toward a rested future. This is political work that is unafraid to step into the light of our dark shared history that is re-creating itself through our individualistic and disconnected delusion of what is really happening to us when we don't rest deeply.

Our liberation is deeply connected to the portal of healing we can tap into when we rest. Wherever our bodies are, we can find rest, ease, and liberation. Part of our decolonizing resides in deprogramming from our brainwashing about rest as our divine right. We are divine. Our bodies are divine and a site of liberation. Wherever our bodies are, we can find, snatch, and center rest.

Tenet 3: Naps provide a portal to imagine, invent, and heal.

This work is a battle cry for being sick and tired of capitalism and white supremacy. A resting place. An alternative and temporary space of joy and freedom. The way both systems view human bodies is evil and unsustainable. No one is being seen clearly within them and instead is viewed as less than human and a machine to be used, abused, and overlooked. This is a meditation on rest as resistance. This is a meditation on rest as reparations. This is a reverberation for my Ancestors. May my deeds in this life please them. May the bass of drums shake liberation from trees. May you join us as we rest.

The Nap Ministry is for resistance and for the softening. The Rest Is Resistance message is for us to hold in our hands, hug while we sleep, and lay down as we think about all the ways our bodies can hold space for liberation. Resting our bodies and minds is a form of reverence. When we honor our bodies via rest, we are connecting to the deepest parts of ourselves. We are freedom-making. What stories are we holding deep inside that are untold and uncovered because we are too exhausted? This rest work is holding space for our memories, our microhistories, and all the things that make us human.

The idea of rest as resistance and rest as reparations can be challenging to distill in a few lines when I am asked to do a quick take. It's counterintuitive to believe rest to be not a place to waste time but instead a generative place of freedom and resistance. We have never learned this in our culture. The thought of not doing, even for a short time, is seen as lazy and unproductive. So an explanation for rest as a form of justice is layered and nuanced. I have learned that one of the most concise and true ways to share the message of rest is to say: "Rest makes us more human. It brings us back to our human-ness." To be more human. To be connected to who and what we truly are is at the heart of our rest movement.

Since the beginning of developing The Nap Ministry, I have repeated, "This is about more than naps," over and over again. I've done this because I realize that it is so easy for us as a culture to attempt to engage with this work from a quick surface level. Social media makes it so seductive to quickly scroll and feel a high from the media presented. It allows for an engagement that lacks depth, slow study, and embodiment. The memes on our page, or what I like to call "propaganda messages," are one of the many tools I use to lay a foundation for us to deprogram from grind culture. But there is always an incomplete understanding when you are engaging on social media because it has been created to be an extension of capitalism. The designers of the platforms wants us there all day scrolling, spending money, and absorbing messages in a fast-paced, disconnected manner.

To truly grasp the heart of the messages, we will have to put down our phones and laptops and rest. We will have to take an intense look at the ways in which grind culture has traumatized us and then begin the lifelong process of healing from this trauma. This work is about more than simply naps and sleep, it is a full unraveling from the grips of our toxic understanding of our self-worth as divine human beings. Grieving in this culture is not done and is seen as a waste of time because grieving is a powerful place of reverence and liberation. A grieving person is a healed person. Can you guess why our culture does not want a healed person in it?

You are worthy of rest. We don't have to earn rest. Rest is not a luxury, a privilege, or a bonus we must wait for once we are burned out. I hear so many repeat the myth of rest being a privilege and I understand this concept and still deeply disagree with it. Rest is not a privilege because our bodies are still our own, no matter what the current systems teach us. The more we think of rest as a luxury, the more we buy into the systematic lies of grind culture. Our bodies and Spirits do not belong to capitalism, no matter how it is theorized and presented. Our divinity secures this, and it is our right to claim this boldly. I'm not grinding ever. I trust the Creator and my Ancestors to always make space for my gifts and talents without needing to work myself into exhaustion.

When we can begin to tap into the deep vessel of who we truly are, so many things would end about oppression. I believe the powers that be don't want us rested because they know that if we rest enough, we are going to figure out what is really happening and overturn the entire system. Exhaustion keeps us numb, keeps us zombie-like, and keeps us on their clock. Overworking and the trauma of burnout continues to degrade our divinity. Once we know and remember we are divine, we will not participate and allow anything into our hearts and minds that is not loving and caring. We would treat ourselves and each other like the tender and powerful beings we are. When I say sleep helps you wake up—it helps you wake up to the truth of who and what you are. And the system doesn't want that. It would crumple under the weight of this power.

Things I know for sure that continue to keep me focused on resting: It's my body, my cells, my skin, my heart, my breath; therefore, I will lovingly center it as the site of my deepest freedom and care. I don't belong to the systems. They cannot have me. I will never donate my body to a system that views it as only a tool for its production. I need you to begin to slowly feel this and to declare that the systems can't have you. It will take deep work but it's imaginative and beautiful work that will be a lifelong process. I am grateful we have a lifetime and our healing needs to not be rushed and urgent. We have a lifetime. We can go slow. We can go deep. We can go into the cracks.

Get up today and tomorrow and think to yourself: "When and where can I find a moment of rest?" You can plot and plan for ten minutes at your desk, thirty minutes of weekend napping, or one minute of resting your eyes. Keep pondering and making space for the time to detox from technology. Listen. What day will you be able to remove one app from your phone in an effort to retain expansiveness for yourself? How will you be able to one day say no to a request that doesn't serve you? To build firm yet caring boundaries that teach us all the meaning of community care? All these things are a form of rest.

Can you find ways to get outdoors in nature, to sky gaze, to ground your feet in the grass, to connect with the land since the land needs healing also? Staring out of the windows on public trains and buses saved my sanity during the height of my exhaustion. White supremacy and capitalism have been using bodies for evil for centuries. They violently push literal bone-crushing labor while ignoring any limits. The body, to those agents of grind culture, is not a divine dwelling and instead a vehicle for profit. Dragging my tired body out onto the streets to walk to the bus stop on my way to an underpaid forty-plus-hours-a-week job. I then would just stare out the window of the moving train, gaining a moment of peace and calm. I connected with the sky, watched the movement of the trees, possibly spotting a favorite bird. Those moments intensely settled my spirit. While I was living these moments, I just knew I felt better. The opportunity to breathe deeply while resting my eyes became a lifeline. I know now that these were moments of rest. I was able to pull back my mind from the grind and settle into my pure existence to just be and to reclaim my body as my own.

The Ministry started while I was daydreaming, napping, and slowing down because my body and my Ancestors told me so. The idea of living in a world but not being part of it is a long-held tradition taught to me by my Ancestors. My grandparents and parents lived it daily and I grew up in Sunday School singing congregational songs with lyrics like: "This joy that I have / The world didn't give it to me / The world didn't give it / The world can't take it away." I am grateful for this politics of refusal and of listening to what we know to be true.

It is risk-taking to do the opposite of what the dominant culture wants. Our work is to slowly and deeply cultivate an expansive inner knowing that trusts our intuition and views rest as a physical and psychological disruption. We can bend time when we rest and I'm grateful for slowness and the embodied work of refusal. The way taking your time and disrupting the dominant culture's need to rush is liberation. To just be, to just deepen into what already is and can never be taken from us is the praxis. We don't need to have our eyes and mouths wide open searching to accomplish more, to be more, to do more. Grind culture has normalized pushing our bodies to the brink of destruction. We proudly proclaim showing up to work or an event despite an injury, sickness, or mental break. We are praised and rewarded for ignoring our body's need for rest, care, and repair. The cycle of grinding like a machine continues and becomes internalized as the only way.

We are made new when we enter the portal of naps. I want you to firmly plant yourself inside your imagination. Take refuge in the beauty and power of community care and our daydreaming. We can build, rest, and usher in a new way that centers liberation and care, no matter what the systems continue to do. Rest is a portal. Silence is a pillow. Sabbath our lifeline. Pausing our compass. Go get your healing. Be disruptive. Push back. Slow down. Take a nap.

Silence and slowness have always inspired my practice as an artist. The role of the artist is to make new things and to resurrect. I am obsessed with community resurrection and individual resurrection. Wherever Spirit is, healing can happen. I'm inspired by invention and the opportunity to craft something new from scratch. I'm interested in remixing. I'm inspired by grief, mourning, and lament. I feel like these places are vulnerable and generative spaces for healing. These states of being must be protected. A reckoning must happen.

The Nap Ministry is a meditation on rest as resistance. It shines a light directly on the power of dismantling the toxic systems that create trauma and terror in our bodies and souls. We center rest as a means for healing and liberation. We believe sleep deprivation is a racial and social justice issue. We must be able to sit with this deep truth: America is not a welcoming place to all bodies. America was built on the backs of Black and Indigenous people who labored without rest for centuries as the country built its economic power. White supremacy became a vehicle to poison the hearts and minds of an entire nation to view human beings as less than divine. Rest is resistance because it is a counternarrative to the script of capitalism and white supremacy for all people.

Resting is a connection and a path back to our true nature. We are stripped down to who we really were before the terror of capitalism and white supremacy. We say no to the systems that see us as simply machines. We resist the lie that we aren't enough. We are enough! We are divine. Our bodies don't belong to these toxic systems. We know better. Our Spirits know better.

Rest meditation practice:

Sit in a chair with your back upright and your feet firmly planted on the floor.
Recline in a chair, on a bed, on a couch, in a hammock, on the floor.
Scan your body and recognize any tension.
Breathe deep.
Imagine a world without limits.
Inhale deeply from your belly, hold for four seconds, exhale slowly.
Repeat.

Tenet 4: Our DreamSpace has been stolen and we want it back. We will reclaim it via rest.

There has been a robbery. DreamSpace Theft. Our DreamSpace has been stolen and we want it back. Each step I take, a hand from my Ancestors reaches up to hold my feet. Holds me close. To lay me down. Reciprocity our salvation. We will prepare a sacred space for you to rest. We want to wrap ourselves in a blanket made of hope. We will rest. Joy is our birthright. Pleasure is our balm. Rest is our resistance.

Social media is robbing us of the archives and memory.

Taking from us the ability to go to the past for guidance, motivation, and grounding. This rest movement is not a trend and is instead the ancient work of liberation. To frame rest as something Black people are finally reclaiming is to erase the history of so many of my Ancestors and those living today who have consistently seen rest as an important part of living and resistance. Audre Lorde, Alice Walker, Harriet Tubman, my grandmother Ora, my mother Jean, the Freedom Riders during the Civil Rights Movement. There is nothing new about Black death, anti-Blackness, and oppression. These things are as old as time and to not see things in totality is causing more trauma.

When I think about the history of the Transatlantic Slave Trade, chattel slavery, and plantation labor, I am stunned by how much we have chosen to forget that capitalism was built from these systems. An experimentation in how to push a human body to a machine-level pace for centuries led by white people dizzy with hate and brainwashed by a system that trained them to look at a divine, human body as property to be owned. This fact by itself is why I will never donate my body to this system and why I navigate my life from a politics of refusal and resistance. My consciousness and Spirit will not allow me to align myself with a system that still owes a debt to my Ancestors. I personally find it disrespectful and of utter disregard to allow myself to be boldly and proudly grinding my body into a state of exhaustion. It stops with me.

I landed at a place of radical faith and a "let the chips fall where they may" attitude when I began experimenting with rest saving my life in 2013 during my first year of divinity school. This personal experience became The Nap Ministry we see today. The more I studied the voices and stories of my Ancestors and went head and body first into listening and communicating with them, I simply could not even begin to re-create the brutality they suffered at the hands of the labor they were forced to participate in on plantations. I vividly remember reading the book *Slave Testimony: Two Centuries of Letters, Speeches, Interviews, and Autobiographies* by John W. Blassingame for six months while in graduate school. I would lay on the couch with this massive collection of archival history and feel rage and power reliving the daily life of an enslaved person. The story of Madison Jefferson, born and enslaved in Virginia as a house servant, who was interviewed in 1841 while living in England. He was a field hand and herder on a plantation with 250 other enslaved people who cultivated tobacco, corn, and hemp. The stories he told of his brother dying while being forced to work in the fields with a head injury rattled me and made me think about all the times capitalism calls for us to ignore our pain and health for the sake of being on the clock. I recalled the trauma of a former boss telling me to come into work after I was in a car accident that sent me to the emergency room with a pinched nerve in my shoulder. In his words, "If you could just muster up the energy to come in for a few hours."

Jefferson goes on in his interview to give details that centered and filled me with rage and empathy in a way I have never experienced before. He recalls the story of receiving fifty lashes for attempting to run away and was chained and placed in a dark dungeon, only to be unchained to work in the fields. As described by Blassingame:

> *"The hours of labor were from daylight till dark regularly, and during busy times, they were frequently at work two hours before the day. Sunday was generally considered a day of rest, but they were frequently employed during the whole of that day in binding wheat, taking up hemp, stemming tobacco and corn. They breakfasted generally at nine o'clock, from half an hour to an hour being allowed, according to the pressure of work—in ordinary times they had a dinner hour and a meal in the evening, but when busy were only allowed two meals, getting an ear of corn or something of that kind in the middle of the day, whilst pursuing their tasks. . . . On the whole, the allowance was very scanty; frequently, Madison says, 'I have cried for hunger after coming from work, and I have seen my brothers and sisters crying round mother for food, and she having none to give them.'"*[1]

The legacy of brutality surrounding labor, sustenance, and survival for those enslaved on plantations and their descendants is striking and why I uplift sleep deprivation as a justice issue.

Grind culture is a collaboration between capitalism and white supremacy. Capitalism is from the plantation. Our current system of labor was made from this paradigm. Knowing this shifted me and must be acknowledged as part of our deprogramming process from grind culture. It is a painful realization, but one we must confront to find our way to healing. What does it feel like to hold this knowledge and to understand you are unconsciously and consciously participating in a system that has its foundation in viewing human bodies as nonhuman machines? What is grind culture doing to our spiritual, mental, and physical health? How does it feel to know your human body is viewed by a capitalist and ableist culture as existing only to make profit? For us to not view our own bodies or the bodies of others as a divine dwelling, the site of liberation and a miracle, is to bow down to the dominant, oppressive culture.

We must see our bodies as a miracle, and a place of reverence where existing in exhaustion is not normal or acceptable. The beauty of resting knows that we are blessed to have a body, to be chosen to be alive, to breathe, to make choices, and to proclaim that our bodies are our own, is a deep practice in care. It is the beginning of a revolution, radical, and a resistance.

★ ★ ★

Rest Is Resistance is a manifesto on the origins of The Nap Ministry, including the main tenets of the Rest Is Resistance movement. The next section of the book will consist of four parts, each a direct call to action:

REST!
DREAM!
RESIST!
IMAGINE!

Illustrated with storytelling and history, and informed by my deep experience in theology, activism, and performance art, it is the story of my Ancestors, my muses, my family, my community, and all that inspired the founding of The Nap Ministry. It's to place into the archives that this work started with me trying to save my own life while basking in the sweetness and power of my Ancestors' lives. It's inspired by American maroons who decided they would never be enslaved on plantations, my grandmother's vegetable garden, my mother's paintings, intergenerational wisdom, kitchen hairstylists, altars constructed outdoors to honor the dead, family reunion T-shirts, art outside the walls of museums, Gwendolyn Brooks, Audre Lorde, bell hooks, James Cone, James Baldwin, Octavia Butler, my granny Ora, who rested her eyes on the couch, Black women, protestors, the Black Church, Black healing music, womanism, my daddy, and to the Ancestors' names I don't know. It is a tenderness, a remixing. Rest is a miracle.

The following invocation has been spoken over the tired bodies of thousands of people who have attended our Collective Napping Experiences in person and virtually. A transmission to open the portal of rest:

The doors of the Nap Temple are open.
Won't you come?
This is an invitation for weary souls to rest.
This is a resistance.
This is a protest.
This is a counternarrative to the lie that we all aren't doing enough.
We are enough.
This is a counternarrative to the lie that our worth is tied to the grind of capitalism and the lie of white supremacy.
You are enough simply by being alive.
Thank you for living.
Thank you for resisting.
Thank you for creating.
Thank you for dreaming.
Thank you for resting.

We believe that our healing can visit us while we are napping.
While we are resting.
While we are sleeping.
While we are slowing down.
We believe that naps provide a dream and visioning space
To invent
To create
To heal.
To imagine
This is what resistance looks like.
Won't you come?
This is a resistance.
This is a protest.

PART ONE

REST!

"Every shut eye ain't sleep. I'm resting my eyes. I'm listening."

—*Ora Caston, my maternal grandmother*

Inspired by: My Ancestors, Intergenerational Wisdom, and Black Liberation Theology

A CALL TO ACTION FOR REST NOW!

I want you to firmly plant yourself inside your imagination.
Take refuge in the beauty and power of our community care.
Take root in our daydreaming.
We can rest, build, and usher in a new way.
We center rest and care no matter what the systems say.
Rest is a portal.
Silence is our pillow.
Hold silence with me now.
Take a deep, full breath.
Hold for four seconds.
Release the shame you feel when resting.
It does not belong to you.

I was once asked in an interview who my guides were for rest growing up as a Black girl in America. With the deepest look of curiosity, the interviewer leaned close, and said, "Who taught you to rest?" I was shook and perplexed, because the question, in all its simplicity, opens up more layers than I could answer in a thirty-minute exchange. No one taught me how to rest by giving intentional guidance or tips. The people in my life found spaces to rest while navigating a racist culture, and they worked themselves into a deadly grind cycle to survive. They straddled the lines between exhaustion and always thriving. They moved mountains with their faith alone and created pathways for invention that I am still uncovering. They resisted every moment by existing in a world that was not welcoming or caring.

I'm proudly from the Midwest. Chicago and its surrounding southern suburbs. City of Big Shoulders, the Windy City. Steel mill and blue-collar energy. Automobile factories. The Lakefront. Skyscrapers, cement, and snow. From Black people who crafted spaces of joy and freedom after fleeing the Jim Crow South during the Great Migration and many who stayed in the South to grow, build, and curate a life centered on community and Spirit. I was held and supported by people who were farmers, cleaners, laborers, factory workers, and contractors. Those who knew how to work from sunup to sundown Monday through Saturday, while Sunday was held as a day of praise and honor to God.

I grew up the child of two African-Americans who were born in the 1950s who, in turn, grew up watching the Civil Rights Movement unfold in front of their eyes. They lived in segregated communities in Chicago and attended integrated high schools where they believed and lived the mantra: *You must work ten times harder than white people to survive and reach success in life.* The call to work exponentially harder has a price.

My dad, Willie Hersey, worked a full-time job as a yardmaster for Union Pacific Railroad and then worked a second full-time job in ministry as an assistant pastor of Robbins Church of God in Christ, a Pentecostal congregation of Black people who believed in casting out demons with your words and inviting the Holy Ghost into every part of your life, including your body. The denomination of the Church of God in Christ, also known as C.O.G.I.C., is a beacon of Black resistance, a Christian organization in the Holiness-Pentecostal tradition. With over six million members worldwide, it is one of the largest Pentecostal churches in the world. It was founded by Bishop Charles H. Mason in 1907 and is made up of predominantly Black people.

I attended my family church from birth to the age of twenty regularly and never saw a white face in the building. The entire land the church sat on, the building, the buses, and the printing press for the church were owned by Black people I knew and loved. This welcoming place of Black autonomy and guidance was my beginning in knowing I am enough right now. It held me up from the inside while an outside system attempted to see my Blackness as criminal.

As the congregation members tarried for hours on the days when the Holy Spirit took over, the final curtain, a display of Black bodies on the floor covered in white sheets, speaking in tongues, as anointed voices and hands on tambourines ushered them into an embodied experience. A healing portal of freedom from whatever prayers were being answered. A moment to test out our freedom in a sacred space created for just us.

The Black Church, and its many contradictions and revelations, holds such tenderness and connection for me and this work. My parents and my maternal grandma Ora, the muse for this work, were deeply guided by its teachings. My mother went into labor with me in church. She stayed for her Sunday School lesson before heading to the hospital. In her words: "Labor goes on for hours, I might as well stay and get my lesson for the strength needed to give birth." So she remained and headed to the hospital three hours later, in no rush, and boosted up by her radical faith and connection to God. After my birth, I was whisked right back into the four walls of our small church that always smelled like fresh butter biscuits with stern wooden pews lined in red velvet fabric.

I grew up here in services three times a week, plus Sunday, with a community of Black radicals who believed in faith so deep that leaping into the unknown felt like dancing to a familiar rhythm. It was our entire lives, everything revolved around it, so Sunday was not a day of rest for my parents, especially my father. It was a day of working tirelessly for the Lord. My father was a mountain of a man. His nicknames were Bear and Big Guy, because his six-foot-five, three-hundred-plus-pound frame would swallow you whole when you received the honor of one of his hugs. A Black militant, preacher, assistant pastor, community organizer, and blue-collar railroad worker for thirty years. A nurturer, dreamer, and resister. He loved freely, giving precious hugs to all he loved and who needed it. He was a friend to so many, a nurturing Spirit.

My father was also always giving me knowledge of how to decolonize. He was considered a Black militant because of his interest in politics and Black liberation, and he taught me from a very young age that the government was solely focused on money. When I was a child of eight, he was teaching me about the demonic ways of capitalism and white supremacy. These lessons were always backed with a message for me to remember who I was. He would repeat, "You are a child of God divinely appointed and chosen to be on Earth." Underneath all his laboring was this imaginative and creative man who had many artistic goals stomped out by grind culture's need for us to work like a machine. But it peeked out in small ways. He was the choir director of our church and was always dancing and singing. He had dreams of being a film director, wanting to be behind the camera to produce and make stories that told our truths.

There wasn't much time for dreaming because he was on the clock twenty-four hours a day. He was the go-to person for any prayer, family emergency, hospital visit, Bible study class and community project created by our church. Many nights, I watched him leap from his soft bed next to my mother to answer late-night phone calls from the congregation. These requests for prayers were fueled by his love of God and his love of Black people. He excelled at holding space. He loved this work, the community, God, and the church. It was his calling, and he gave every ounce of energy to it, his family, and his main railroad job. I never remember my dad not working constantly or not being involved in helping others and the community. I watched my father get up every morning at four a.m. He would drag himself out of bed to sit at the kitchen table to read three newspapers, study his Bible, and pray silently. He would do this for almost two hours before he needed to leave for work at six. I remember asking, "Why do you get up so early when you don't have to be at work until later?" He replied, "I want to have a few moments in the day that belong to just me before I clock in." A moment to be human and to settle into his body to connect with his Creator. A moment to just be before going into his railroad job to clean train cars. He eventually worked his way to be the supervisor of the entire train yard. For decades, he was the only Black person in a management role and suffered consistent racial discrimination and daily microaggressions. He tried to protect my siblings and me from the trauma he endured there, but many days I overheard him telling my mama about how intense it was becoming. "They have been calling me a nigger to my face and behind my back. It's rough." For thirty years, he attempted to prove himself with overtime constantly and perfect attendance, all while being an assistant pastor, choir director, and community organizer. He juggled so much to provide a loving and stable home to us, but there is something that lurks beneath when we are living in a system founded on our labor to prove our worth as human beings.

His love of community and God fueled him endlessly, but the toxic side to this passion was his overworking, exhaustion, and lack of caring for his body. He gave everything he had to others, while his physical health suffered greatly. The link between sleep deprivation and stress to the development of chronic diseases is real. He had major health issues at a young age: diabetes, obesity, high blood pressure, heart disease, and sleep apnea. An internalized grind culture set things in motion for an early death at fifty-five. After a triple bypass heart surgery that he survived with flying colors to repair arteries seventy-five percent blocked, his diabetes complicated the healing process and his body simply gave out under all the stress, lack of care, lack of boundaries, and expectations.

I remember watching my father die. My community right next to me for the entire journey. The entire church congregation and our large family caring for every demand during his recovery time at the hospital and at home. What seemed like hundreds of people coming to bring my mother food, run errands for my father, sitting and talking with him bedside, bringing him oranges, sneaking in deli sandwiches and anything else he could imagine a craving for. Along with the material things came the prayers, the hugs, the Bible verses read aloud, the laying on of hands. There was intense spiritual energy around. I could literally feel the presence of God in the house. In my heart. As the weeks went on he got weaker and it was later discovered that an infection was present where the stitches to close his chest remained. It had spread to his blood and he was back in the hospital surrounded by community. I watched the pastors, deacons, and prayer warrior missionaries pray over him with the intensity of ten thousand blazing suns. The community became so overwhelming that the hospital requested we create a visitor schedule since the room and hallway outside his room was packed daily. This went on for weeks, until one evening my father peacefully left this realm.

The nurses in the intensive care unit were so kind. Angels on Earth floating in green scrubs. Tiptoeing around us like we were porcelain figures in an expensive department store. They let us sit and stand there for hours touching his body. I didn't think twice about kissing his face, holding his still-warm hands, and rubbing his hair. I wanted to hug him around his neck, squeezing with interlaced fingers like stone. My mama sat on a low stool, dazed and confused. The man she loved for forty years covered in thick double white sheets up to his neck. She slowly removed the sheets from his right foot and just began rubbing it slowly. The rubbing turned to a gentle massage that I lovingly prayed would wake the dead. Softly she whispered, "Please Willie, don't leave us." But he was already gone and we three women, my older sister Camie, my mama, and me stood around this mountain of a man weeping and kissing.

I don't remember leaving the ICU room, but when I did look up I was in the small waiting room adjacent to the large heavy steel doors of the intensive care ward. Standing before me were close to fifty people. I could identify most of the faces but then they all began to blend into the air. Everyone was crying and looked shell-shocked. War veterans on a leave. I felt weak in the knees. My head began to spin. I actually thought I was going to faint. Fainting would've been welcomed right then. I wanted to hit my head on the end of that random wheelchair sitting in the hallway and I wanted it to be blood and I wanted to die, too. I wanted to go with him. The grief was too much to bear. As soon as I snapped back into reality after a few minutes, I could feel my favorite uncle, Lance, holding me around my waist and carefully placing me on the floor, my back sliding up against the beige wall, with him kneeling next to me saying, "I got you, niecey. It's gonna be okay. I'm right here." He sat next to me and just held my hand.

Grind culture killed my father and is killing us physically and spiritually. Sleep deprivation is a public health issue and a racial justice issue. There is a large body of research that points to the sleep gap that exists between Black Americans and white Americans.

"The researchers found that during this period, Black respondents were consistently more likely to have very short sleep or short sleep, compared with their white counterparts."[1] The need for my dad to sleep deeply was not a priority in our culture and I observed in real time the consequences of this reality.

As I held silence for a few long minutes staring at the interviewer, I couldn't give a clear answer to the inquiry: "Who taught you to rest?" Maybe that's the reason for this curiosity I have with rest now. The lack of an open pathway to rest has never been given to most living in a capitalist system. There is no blueprint or cookie-cutter way to get to our liberation. We rest to find our way through. A refusal. The crafting of a Third Space. Fugitivity.

What has been repeated to me over and over again by people who are newly exposed to the rest message is: "I wish I could rest but I just don't know how to nap. It feels impossible." Consistently for six years, this has been the mantra shared with me by thousands. It is firm evidence that we as a culture don't have clarity about what rest is and can be. These limitations and confusions have been created in us. We are born knowing how to rest and listen to what our bodies need. It's second nature and an inner knowing. Infants and children follow their body cues and, without doing so, would not survive. This inner knowing is slowly stolen from us as we replace it with disconnection. We have been bamboozled and led astray by a culture without a pause button. We are barely surviving from our sleep deprivation, worker exploitation, and exhaustion. We must rest.

Rest is not what you may automatically think of. Most of my time I've led the Ministry has been spent opening to this reality: Everything we believe we know about rest is false. Because we are in a constant state of unraveling from the lies and socialization of grind culture, we must be intentional about reimagining what we believe rest is and can be for our lives. We must ask ourselves the following questions and more: If I have been consistently exposed and brainwashed by the violence of grind culture since birth, do I really know what rest feels like? Do I have a model or guide for what it feels like to be rested while living inside a capitalist system? What would it feel like to be consistently rested? What does exhaustion look like for me? Am I navigating the world from a constant state of exhaustion? Who was I before the terror of the toxic systems? Who do I want to be? What have you been told about your worth and existence? How do you make space to transcend the confines of a system that prays to the call of "profit over people"?

My commitment to saving my own life via rest is rooted in my commitment and study of womanism. I learned of womanism while in graduate school. I am now aware that I have been a womanist most of my life. The white feminism that I was fed by public schools as a child and as a young woman in college always felt insufficient and dishonest. I remember asking a history teacher in junior high that if women got the right to vote in 1920, did it include Black women? He ignored my question by saying he would get back to it, but never did. There is never an answer when you are erasing.

The term *womanist* was coined by Alice Walker in 1983. It appeared in her book *In Search of Our Mothers' Gardens* and defines a womanist as "Wanting to know more and in greater depth than is considered 'good' for one. Committed to survival and wholeness of entire people, male and female."[2] For me, the beauty of womanism is its holistic view of change. It centers the deep shared commitment Black women have to their family and community. Unlike white feminism, womanism holds space for race, class, and gender and understands the family and community of a Black woman are collaborators in the struggle for liberation. It seeks balance and flexibility. Womanism is what allows me to see rest as a tool for liberation. A global movement seeking to repair all that has been broken by capitalism, white supremacy, and patriarchy. I know that saving my own life from the exhaustion of racism, poverty, and sexism made space for all, no matter their race, to also begin the dismantling process from these systems. My view of Black liberation being a balm for all our humanity is heavily influenced by womanism. I understand rest to be a spiritual practice because I am a womanist.

My study and commitment to womanism informs much of my curiosity of the visions of a well-rested future. I know that my visualizations of what a world without capitalism and oppression looks like is based on something I have never experienced in this lifetime. It is dreamwork and alchemy. My personal work is to more fully understand the process of transformation while being clear about the realities we exist in. I am always pondering: "What will a well-rested world for all hold? What will be the elements?

Will everyone get free from grind culture? Have we been tangled up in the muck of the grind for so long that we may never come up for air?"

The book *Making a Way Out of No Way: A Womanist Theology* by Monica Coleman gave voice to what I couldn't fully articulate, but have felt since the work of rest has received greater attention:

> *"Not all evil can be overcome in this world, and yet a postmodern womanist theology maintains hope in the struggle to creatively and constructively respond to it. Sometimes feelings of discord are the result of the conflicts in this world. Sometimes liberation is not possible, but survival and quality of life are. All-encompassing health, wholeness, unity, and salvation are never fully attained in this world. As we constantly become, we are constantly vulnerable to evil and constantly capable of overcoming it. In postmodern womanist theology, salvation is an activity. Each new moment brings possibilities in both directions. A postmodern womanist theology strives for tangible representations of the good. The good includes justice, equality, discipleship, quality of life, acceptance and inclusion."*[3]

My personal attempt at disrupting capitalism and white supremacy by resting does appear to be a goal with an unattainable end, because as I evolve and heal, evil is always present. A valuable question is: How can we afford to rest when the colonizing Empire we live within daily continues to rage on and grow stronger? The Empire continues to morph, plan, and strategize to maintain power. The words of Monica Coleman above pull back the veils we have all been wearing as part of living in a toxic system. We believe that we can heal and reimagine new ways of living by re-creating the evil and abuse taught to us. Yes, the system continues raging and destroying but we will not be able to tap into spaces of freedom, joy, and rest by pushing our precious bodies and minds in abusive ways. To rest is to creatively respond to grind culture's call to do more. It's the possibility of rest, reparations, resurrection, and repair that holds us like a warm, soft blanket.

How do we make the impossible possible? How do we process the theft of our DreamSpace and our humanity? Where do we place the grief of our treatment under grind culture? How can we begin to understand how white supremacy strips us of our connection to Spirit? How can we begin to explain the spiritual deficiency that occurs when you follow and uplift white supremacist thinking? How do we transform grief to power? Lay and rest in these questions. We don't have to have a complete answer to everything right now. We don't have to know everything. We don't have to be everything. We don't have to do everything. There is space for the unknown. There is space for curiosity and mystery.

There is space to just allow rest to settle and answer the questions for us.

Everything we know about rest has been tainted by the brainwashing from a white supremacist, capitalist system. As a culture, we don't know how to rest, and our understanding of rest has been influenced by the toxicity of grind culture. We believe rest is a luxury, privilege, and an extra treat we can give to ourselves after suffering from exhaustion and sleep deprivation. Rest isn't a luxury, but an absolute necessity if we're going to survive and thrive. Rest isn't an afterthought, but a basic part of being human. Rest is a divine right. Rest is a human right. We come into the world prepared to love, care, and rest. The systems kill us slowly via capitalism and white supremacy. Rest must interrupt. Like hope, rest is disruptive, it allows space for us to envision new possibilities. We must reimagine rest within a capitalist system.

For many, rest feels elusive and there is no model for rest in our culture. We must create the model and dream up new ways of being. It is our work to reimagine rest for ourselves. We do this by tapping into the infinite imagination we have as divine beings. We slowly take our time to go underneath the many layers of trauma we have experienced individually and collectively in this violent system. We lay down literally and figuratively.

Why we are not resting

We are not resting because we are still connecting to our rest in a capitalist, trendy, consumer-driven way. The way we have been trained under a capitalist system. Our work is not about a one-day-only event, where leaving your homes is necessary to rest in a fancy retreat center or hotel. This work is about a slow unraveling that will require our participation for our entire lives. It is a cultural shift, rooted in an embodiment lens. This means that we must actively practice, engage, and push back against the dominant culture. We must snatch and integrate rest in the quiet, loud, mundane, and full moments of our lives daily. We must remain committed to building community and go into the deepest cracks to gather and care for anyone left behind. Treating each other and ourselves with care isn't a luxury, but an absolute necessity if we're going to thrive. Resting isn't an afterthought, but a basic part of being human.

We must make space for rest in small and large ways. We want it to become a daily practice that is reimagined by you. You are the expert of your own body. Your body is yours and knows the way. Our embodiment will happen in our bodies daily and in our Spirits forever. In the spirit of Audre Lorde who said, "Revolution is not a one-time event," we intentionally don't participate in social media challenges around naps, or in trendy one-off events that don't include intensive education centering Black liberation and history. We must uplift the meticulous depths of what decolonizing and deprogramming truly looks like. The Rest Is Resistance framework also does not believe in the toxic idea that we are resting to recharge and rejuvenate so we can be prepared to give more output to capitalism. What we have internalized as productivity has been informed by a capitalist, ableist, patriarchal system. Our drive and obsession to always be in a state of "productivity" leads us to the path of exhaustion, guilt, and shame. We falsely believe we are not doing enough and that we must always be guiding our lives toward more labor. The distinction that must be repeated as many times as necessary is this: We are not resting to be productive. We are resting simply because it is our divine right to do so. That is it! Rest in this proclamation for a moment.

Our rest is centered on connecting and reclaiming our divinity, given to us by our birth. The concept of filling up your cup first, so you can have enough in it to pour to others feels off balance. It reeks of the capitalist language that is now a part of our daily mantras. Language like "I will sleep when I am dead," "Rise and grind," "While they sleep, I grind," "If it doesn't make money, it doesn't make sense," "Wake up to hustle," and many more. The cup metaphor also is most often geared toward women, who, because of patriarchy and sexism, carry the burden of labor. Marginalized women, specifically Black and Latina women, make up the largest group of laborers in a capitalist system. Our labor historically has been used to make the lives of white women less hectic and more relaxed. So when I hear and see this "filling your cup" language repeated on memes on social media and in the larger wellness community, I realize that our view of rest is still burdened with the lies of grind culture. I propose that the cups all be broken into little pieces, and we replace pouring with resting and connecting with our bodies in a way that is centered on experimentation and repair. I don't want to pour anymore. It is time to begin the dismantling of the cult of busyness one person at a time. One heart at a time. One body at a time.

Our resting is not a one-time event because to disrupt grind culture there must be a global mind shift that is relentless, constant, subversive, and intentional. To push back against the machine of white supremacy and capitalism, even for ten minutes, is a miracle. This will look like rest being available to everyone. No matter your income, physical ability, sexuality, gender, geographic location, or access. It is not connected to consumerism, capitalism, or the never-ending goal of many to go viral. The Nap Ministry and our Rest Is Resistance framework are a total pause on everything we have ever been taught about wellness from a white supremacist, capitalist lens. We don't want more of the same and are fully dedicated to interrupting and cultivating infinite imagination that will release our DreamSpace.

* * *

Sunday, May 21, 2017. Atlanta, Georgia. Our first Collective Napping Experience came to me without trying. The way it came together feels pulled together by Spirit. I was finishing up my graduate studies and began speaking to those in my artistic circle in Atlanta about my next steps in my career. I shared I was applying to jobs in chaplaincy at hospitals, schools, and community centers. I was attempting to discern my next steps for a career that was aligned with a justice path. I had very little money, was exhausted from the humiliating cycle of interviewing for jobs, and had only told a few people about my idea of creating an art piece on rest. Randomly, people kept telling me about this woman named Charlie who had this large space in Atlanta that I could use for an event. I never followed through until the third person emailed me. I finally called and set up a meeting to see the space knowing I had no money to pay any rental fees, no staff to help curate, or afford the cost of materials to design the space into a comfortable space for sleep. I went anyway. Once there, I walked into a room that felt like a magical oasis created for sleep with a soft carpeted floor, warm lighting, extra-large floor pillows, a tea bar, and light fabric hanging from the ceilings. It was already made for rest. As I sat and drank tea and toured the space, a feeling of guidance and connection poured over me. Charlie told me I could use the space anytime, day or night, and she wouldn't accept any money from me. In her words, "It's a place of experimentation. Use it." So, without a job that would pay my bills and while still searching for work after spending almost four years studying in seminary, The Nap Ministry gathered forty people into a room to rest and hold space for healing and education in what was to be a one-night-only event. I never got hired at any of the jobs I applied to and stepped full force into this work after this event. My commitment to honoring my own body, community care, and the remembrance of my Ancestors came together as if my Ancestors themselves were blowing wind under my wings and holding my hand, offering rest as a gift for the world.

The centerpiece of this work began as and will always be our Collective Napping Experiences. Curating in-person and virtual spaces for us to rest together, to hold space for each other and to enter the portal of rest as a sacred act. One of the objectives is for each person to gain hands-on tools to engage with rest whenever and wherever. This mandate is why all our Collective Napping Experiences are free and blend intensive education and embodiment experiences. We center the issue of accessibility and try to answer the following questions: What becomes of the people who cannot afford to be away from their home for twenty-four hours or a weekend? What about the people who have children and no childcare? How will those who are homebound due to disability participate in a retreat that requires travel? What about the introverts who don't want to be around groups? How will the rest continue after they return home? Why are their homes and communities seen as a place that needs leaving behind to rest? Are we simply providing a comfy bed and soothing music without a framework rooted in liberation? Why isn't our rest powerful enough to be accessed anytime and anywhere?

I believe this work will not happen in the fake luxurious ways that we believe rest must happen. It will not happen away from our communities, held up in expensive hotels and retreat centers. If the message of rest is to be truly for all and a full-on decolonizing moment, it must be life-altering and within our own communities, homes, workspaces, religious institutions, academic spaces, and, most importantly, in our minds. I don't believe we will get to freedom from grind culture by doing more of the same and aligning ourselves with any corporate wellness message that does not get to the root of the issue. To not illuminate the systems making us unwell is to bypass the heart and soul of justice work. To uplift rest from a community care ethic is to interrupt the dominant culture while giving the power back to the people where it belongs. Our rest praxis calls first for a mental shift that does not have an end date. We will be healing from our brainwashing from grind culture forever. We must be vigilant about the ways in which we will flow in and out of the grips of grind culture. There will be days when you will be pulled back into the system and will find yourself spinning, dizzy with the effects of hyperproductivity. The work is to first gain deep awareness that the pace at which this culture is functioning is not normal or sustainable. This understanding offers an invitation for the collective pilgrimage we are on as we attempt to disrupt and push back against a system that has no pause button. Stay here for a while. Stay in the space of knowing that you are not a failure, inadequate or unworthy because you are tired and want to rest. There is no need to now attempt to figure this all out today and to be totally on board to embracing rest in a way that doesn't feel right to you. This protest against grind culture is for you to create in your own body. Your body is yours. Its uniqueness and stories it has to tell are yours. A community call toward rest as a form of activism is a call to slow down and listen and care. It is an empowered place fueled by the shared goal of becoming more human. We are not machines. We are not on Earth to fulfill the desires of an abusive system via our exhaustion.

We are not resting because social media has stolen our ability to exist without it. A perfect plan to keep us distracted and addicted. The algorithms guiding our every move, putting unnecessary pressure on many to post, retweet, hashtag, and grow their platforms obsessively. I have never been concerned with the follower count on our social media pages. I am very concerned and focused on using social media as one of the many tools at our reach to further deprogram those who have the desire to disrupt grind culture in their lives. I don't want people to connect to our rest work based on an algorithm. I want people to connect because Spirit sent them and, once there, the idea of rest gave comfort and peace.

We as a culture spend countless hours a day on social media with numerous studies naming it as a digital addiction. '"Thirty-two percent of teen girls said that when they felt bad about their bodies, Instagram made them feel worse," the authors wrote in a presentation obtained by the *Wall Street Journal*. "They often feel 'addicted' and know that what they're seeing is bad for their mental health but feel unable to stop themselves."'[4]

When I take a digital Sabbath away from social media, I come back feeling smarter, less anxious, and tapped into an expansive energy I was unable to access while scrolling every day. My body is an antenna for infinite ideas and inventions when I disconnect from the energy of technology and when I rest. One of the best ways to test out how silence is a form of rest is to plan a social media detox. For those who are attached to your phones, start off small at first by blocking out two to four hours to be off all social media sites. By deleting the apps off the phone, or placing your phone in another room, tucked away in a drawer, you can increase your chances of finding a natural rhythm without the voices and noise that social media provides. Even if your timeline is curated to only include joyful, thought-provoking, and encouraging messages, detoxing is still necessary and valuable. Your mind needs space for silence. Space to process what it is feeling without the participation of others. Your brain needs deep, consistent sleep, rest, and silence to make new connections, for memory retention, and to download. Our mental health is strengthened when we are away from the glare of computer screens and not absorbing the thoughts and ideas of thousands of people during one day of endless scrolling. Can you imagine a few hours a day of not being connected to your phones or email inboxes? What feelings rise inside when you imagine it? What if this day was extended to a full day or a full week? A month? What would you replace the hours of online engagement with? Could a hobby be cultivated during this time that could give you pleasure? Would you have more time to daydream, rest, nap? Would you go to bed earlier? Does it feel stressful to think about not having your phone nearby? What has the pervasive nature of social media and cell phones done to our quiet time?

I critique the internet for the ways in which it has quickly shifted—after all, it has only been accessible for the masses as a part of daily living for twenty-five years. Social media now is a space of dependency. We will not be able to fully get to a rested state if we don't greatly reduce our use of social media. I know this is a wild and bold statement in a culture solely oriented toward more automation, technological innovation, and digital living. Currently, the Metaverse has become real. Millions of people are waiting anxiously for this digital world to materialize so they can move in and stay. If we aren't already distracted, exhausted, and disembodied, this major disruption to a physical world could be yet another violent piece to the traumatizing culture of grinding. As a person totally focused on our Spirits, souls, minds, and bodies, I am worried about the role the Metaverse will play in an already sleep-deprived and disconnected world. There are too many ways to ignore the deep inner knowing, intuition, and divine wisdom that exists in us from birth already. To exist daily over time in a space of increased virtual experiences will have a lasting effect on our ability to push back against capitalism and white supremacy. The idea of ownership, personal connections, entertainment, and education existing in a centralized virtual world opens up the possibility for us to never truly rest and for the manipulation of capitalism to welcome us in like a sheep headed to slaughter. We must be clear and committed right now to keeping the veils removed from our eyes as capitalism moves in aggressive and unique ways. Resting must become our focus.

Living our lives in virtual spaces sounds alluring to some and, for many communities, the opportunity to connect is a lifeline and revolutionary. It opens places not readily available or accessible. It holds intense support, resources, and motivation. It is a beautiful balancing act to hold space for two or more things being true at the same time. It is freedom. The digital world and social media are places of connection for many, and also are places of toxicity, disconnection, and exhaustion. They can be both and there doesn't have to be tension around it. It simply is and it offers an opportunity for us to live into the nuance and be hyperaware of the energy and time we use for it. We must detox intentionally and often if we are to find rest. Without examining the hold social media has over our lives, we will never be able to push any rest movement forward. It's simply not possible because social media is an extension of capitalism. It is a marketing tool. The developers and designers of our current platforms are not leaders of a billion-dollar industry simply so we can all stay connected to our family, friends, and communities. It is used for this successfully by many, but please remember it is not the goal for capitalists. The goal is to keep you scrolling long enough that you become a consumer. The goal is for you to buy, buy some more, and stay on as long as possible until that happens. We are not resting because we are online for hours and hours a day, distracted and exhausted. This is why we must view rest as the ultimate disruption of capitalism's tricks and plans. An exodus and intentional detox from these platforms are the North Star for our rest practice.

For this ethic of community care to multiply, we need to be resting always in our quiet moments, in our busy moments, in our bedrooms, in our bathrooms, in our schools, on our porches, in our neighborhoods, in our cities, and in our minds. The beautiful interruption of rest needs to happen now. We cannot wait for the perfect opportunity, the perfectly curated events, or the perfect moment for us to leave our capitalist world. For our rest to be generative we must be always leaping from an anticapitalist agenda. We must leave the memes on social media and the hot takes that come from the co-opting and parroting that happen in the fraudulent, clout-driven world that is the internet. When we rest, we are pushing back against a system created on plantations, with a central belief that we must have money, a fancy mattress, and the allure of individualism for our rest to be generative. This is a lie. We must slowly unravel daily to understand that our liberation, freedom, and everything we need is already within us. It doesn't matter how much money we make, how much time we can get off work, and how many vacations we take.

What matters is that in our hearts and souls we have decided to refuse and not wait until we have enough or have the perfect number of external things for our rest to be approved by the larger system. We do not need the participation of grind culture to be able to claim our bodies and time as our own. Black people have a direct connection to the brutality of capitalism. Our bodies were America's first capital and our rest and DreamSpace are stolen constantly. The legacy of white supremacy on our journey toward rest must be viewed as a life-shifting proposal. We must rest like our lives depend on it, because it does.

The offering of James Cone and his creation of Black Liberation theology grounded my development of The Nap Ministry. The message of rest as a message of reparations and liberation to Black people is firmly planted in Cone's scholarship. This work is intentionally secular but I cannot help but be inspired by those leanings, which inspire me as a person. I am deeply inspired by Black religious thought and Black spirituality. The framework of Rest Is Resistance is very personal to me and its origins come from me saving my own life from exhaustion, while tapping into the imaginative spaces of refusal given to me by my Ancestors.

In Cone's classic book, *A Black Theology of Liberation,* originally published in 1970, Cone speaks about the nuances of Black history and how our experiences help us to navigate a system committed to not seeing us. This lack of seeing us affects how we rest: "If black theology is going to speak to the condition of black persons, it cannot ignore the history of white inhumanity committed against them. But black history is more than what whites did to blacks. More importantly black history is black persons saying no to every act of white brutality. Contrary to what whites say in their history books, black power is not new."[5] There is already power and with that power I have said no to capitalism and to any and everything working to degrade my divinity. I see the brilliance and miracle of human beings. We are not machines. This work would not be possible without my deep study and love of Black Liberation theology. It has taught me from a very early age that God cares for me no matter my skin color, economic status, or ability. I learned as a young child from the Black Church that my Black body was not criminal and instead a deep reflection of God. Listening to my dad and other Black preachers holler a message of Black liberation from the pulpit shaped me and has allowed me to view white supremacy and capitalism as demonic forces that don't deserve to rob me. I was taught that God was on the side of the oppressed and any theology that spread anything different was not a true Christianity. To read the Biblical text from a lens of Black liberation opens up doors and removes veils that have boosted up my self-worth deeply from the inside. It's why I have such radical faith and a rooted belief in what I am born to do. I know that I was not born to simply exhaust myself inside a violent system. I know that if I never check another item off my to-do list, I am still worthy and loved by God and my Ancestors. Black Liberation theology taught me this and continues to be a burning flame in my hands and heart as it lights the paths before me when everything is dark. Because of this foundational understanding, the work of The Nap Ministry has grown. My commitment to seeing every toxic system that interferes and degrades the divinity of myself and every human on the planet dismantled is because the bamboozlement of grind culture has been revealed via rest and slowing down. We must rest, heal, and resist together.

I have spent the entirety of my life as the Nap Bishop answering this question: "Is The Nap Ministry just for Black people?" The question itself stems from a white supremacist mindset that refuses to accept this truth: Black liberation is a balm for all humanity and this message is for all those suffering from the ways of white supremacy and capitalism. Everyone on the planet, including the planet itself, is indeed suffering from these two systems. The way in which this suffering manifests for each group is unique to their history. White people have had their humanity stripped from them via white supremacy. They are spiritually deficient and blinded by the idea that they are superior to other divine human beings. The lineage of terror, violence, enslavement resides in these bodies and hearts. Also, what does it help me to live in a world where I am the only one who is liberated from the grips of grind culture? I will still have to engage and collaborate with those still bound up and moving from a place of fear and urgency. My freedom from grind culture is intimately tied up in the healing and liberation of all those around me. Community care and a full communal unraveling is the ultimate goal for any justice work, because without this we will be left vulnerable to the lie of toxic individualism. Our justice leaders have been screaming this from the rooftops for centuries and yet our toxic individualism, residing in an exhausted, brainwashed mind, continues to ignore this life-giving wisdom.

We are all connected by virtue of living in the same communities, working in shared office spaces, engaging with each other in schools, on streets, and as we travel. The rigid idea that justice work centering Blackness, born from a lens of Black liberation, is only for Black people is limiting and false. Black liberation is a global shift for an entire world bamboozled by the lies of capitalism and white supremacy. The belief that what one does and experiences does not affect everyone around them is a myth and disease that Americans severely suffer from. When we don't take our own rest while holding space for others around us to rest, we are functioning like the systems we want to gain freedom from. I battle and navigate this daily as I engage with corporations, institutions, and individuals constantly ignoring my workflow boundaries, requesting work from me even while on an announced sabbatical, and requesting my labor for free. I am amazed at how many well-meaning people interested in this work aggressively push and micromanage our interactions. Because grind culture is a curriculum that has been forced on us and reinforced through corporate and academic culture, it is always present. When we function thinking only of ourselves and believing we can do it alone, we create harm and create a container for more exhaustion.

Fannie Lou Hamer, a freedom fighter and civil rights icon, and Dr. Martin Luther King Jr. both had this interconnectedness idea as a central organizing principle. Their quotes: "No one is free until we are all free" and "No one is free until everybody's free," identical in energy and truth. Black freedom fighters have understood deeply the reality of crafting a loving community as a justice practice. bell hooks, in her classic text, *all about love,* reaches back to the words of Dr. Martin Luther King Jr. in the chapter "Community: Loving Communion." She writes: "Writing about the need to bridge the gulf between the rich and the poor, Martin Luther King, Jr., preached: 'All men [and women] are caught in an inescapable network of mutuality, tied in a single garment of destiny. Whatever affects one directly affects all indirectly.' This gulf is bridged by the sharing of resources. Every day, individuals who are not rich but who are materially privileged make a choice to share with others. Mutual giving strengthens community."[6] Mutual and collective rest disrupts, interrupts, and heals. Our collective resting coordinated with traveling deep within our hearts begins the process of dismantling capitalism, white supremacy, racism, homophobia, ableism, and patriarchy.

While it is the work of everyone on the planet to disrupt and push back against white supremacy and capitalism, Blackness and Black people are the foundation and North Star for my experimentation with rest as a form of resistance. They have charted the path for rest and refusal for me in deeply spiritual and metaphysical ways. There is no Rest Is Resistance movement without Blackness. Anyone attempting to create and expand on our rest message must reach deep into the cracks to study and uplift Black liberation. It is the North Star for an exhausted world. Anyone co-opting our message without crediting our work and the scholarship of Black people are caught up deeply in the grips of grind culture, and could not possibly be embodying rest. They are to be carefully critiqued as an agent of capitalism and white supremacy thinking.

We are in crisis. This rest movement is not some cute and frivolous idea but instead an intentional disruption against very violent systems. It has the potential to save lives and restore bodies and minds. It is healing work that will not be easy. It is a resistance wrapped in softness and bold enough to stand up to the powers that be and quietly and loudly proclaim, "We Will Rest!"

This work is also about rage. My tender rage about what the systems have done to my body, my Ancestors' bodies, my family, and the entire culture. This work is a tender rage originating from ancestral rage that has been unspoken and hidden. When I think about grind culture, and what it has done to my own body, I deepen into my resistance. When I spend time processing the manipulation, the scam, and declaration by grind culture that our bodies do not belong to us and instead belong to systems seeking domination and wealth, it enrages and saddens me. Collective rest is not about just changing our individual lives but shifting the entire paradigm of culture. Our disruption of capitalism and white supremacy via rest is to pull back the veil and get behind the curtain to see everything that has been told to us about rest, labor, sleep, leisure, and care has been a lie.

When I was growing up, I was forced to play my role in an unrealistic standard of perfection at school, work, and church. This "do more" belief was passed on to me and my siblings by my parents and every adult in our lives, including our teachers. I remember being in elementary school doing homework and my father lovingly telling me that I had to always work harder in life because the world didn't see me as capable, even though I was smart. There was a sense of doing more, just to be seen as equal, that was always lingering in the air around me. A higher standard of excellence sitting in the pit of your stomach that made it easy to push past the normal pace of life. There were times when I was deeply caught up in the machine-level pace of living that our culture calls for and I knew it did not feel normal. Every time this happened, I felt something was wrong. My body could never truly relax or pause. My mind was always going as I constantly thought about the next thing I had to do, the newest bill to be paid, the hours I had to work this week to save money, the side hustles I could create to pay for an unexpected expense. Every single moment of the day was dedicated to what I could accomplish. True liberation to me is to not be constantly attempting to prove our worth and ticking off to-do lists. To just be.

I love the idea and concept of simply existing and just being for Black folks. The idea of "you gotta be better than those before you," Black excellence, and the never-ending cycle to be an inspiration and "model" is tiring, unsustainable, and steeped in white supremacy, respectability politics, and wrecks our self-esteem as Black folks. What if we simply saw our birth and living and breathing and connection with ourselves and our families as enough? This deep knowing of our divinity without doing another thing. This is what I hope for so many of us. I give thanks to my father, my closest

Ancestor, for showing me how to snatch moments of rest while living within a capitalist system.

This work is about more than naps. Resistance in our Rest Is Resistance framework means we rest no matter what the systems say. We reimagine rest for ourselves. We craft spaces of physical, spiritual, and psychological rest to disrupt and push back against white supremacy and capitalism. It is a lifelong deprogramming. A mind shift and an ethos that engages with rest as a tool for liberation. The body has information. The trauma response is to keep going and to never stop. Grinding keeps us in a cycle of trauma; rest disturbs and disrupts this cycle. Rest is an ethos of reclaiming your body as your own. Rest provides a portal for healing, imagination, and communication with our Ancestors. We can work things out in a DreamSpace. What miraculous moments are you missing because you aren't resting?

How to rest

There is no rush. There is no urgency. Unravel from the lies of white supremacy culture. Rest is a meticulous love practice. How will it be possible to rest in a capitalist system? What will resting look like in the reality of our daily lives? How can you pay bills and rest? What is the first step to begin? This work will not be easy.

It must be said right from the beginning that resting,

slowing down, napping, and sleeping are not what grind culture expects of us. It will truly be a resistance since the systems make us hard and machine-like. Rest keeps us tender and there is power in our tenderness and care. We will have to slow down enough to listen to what our hearts and bodies want to share with us. Our lives are a beautiful experiment in curiosity and creation. We can craft a life outside of toxic systems. Collective care, imagination, and rest are so vital to our liberation. Without them, we will not make it.

WHO IS RESTING FOR:

Rest is for the weary, for the hard workers, for those trying to make a way, for those making a way yet still suffering from disconnection, for those wondering when they will be able to get a full night's sleep, for those thinking they aren't worthy enough to sleep and don't deserve rest because they've been socialized to believe this, for the faith workers and those out on the front lines, to those raising children and trying to do what's best, to the entrepreneur, to the unemployed, to the blue collar worker, to the white collar worker, to those brainwashed by a system that has taught you aren't enough unless you produce. Rest is for all of us. A global movement for all to be able to tap back into our divinity. Rest is our divine right. It is not a luxury or privilege.

Rest is as natural as breathing and waking up. Rest is

part of our nature. Resting is about getting people back to their truest selves. To what they were before capitalism robbed you of your ability to just be. Rest is anything that slows you down enough to allow your body and mind to connect in the deepest way. We must be focused on knowing that our bodies and our worth are not connected to how many things we can check off a list. You can begin to create a "Not-To-Do List" as you gain the energy to maintain healthy boundaries. Our opportunity to rest and reimagine rest is endless. There is always time to rest when we reimagine.

Resting is for everyone caught up in the web of grind culture. We must never forget that grind culture is a sinister collaboration between capitalism and white supremacy. When viewed from this lens, we are all caught up in these toxic systems. Born, raised, and trained from birth under the same curriculum. Those who are wealthy, as well as those who are poor, are caught up in the spiritual deficiency that occurs when you are tied to a system like capitalism in any way. We are all harmed in unique ways. This fact is supported by studying history.

Some places to begin:

1. Detox from social media weekly, monthly, or more.
2. Begin to heal the individual trauma you have experienced that makes it difficult for you to say no and maintain healthy boundaries.

3. Start a daily practice in daydreaming.
4. Accept that there is no quick fix, magic bullet, or instant change.
5. Slowly accept you have been brainwashed. Your socialization in a capitalist culture makes this true. Begin to deprogram by accepting this truth.
6. Slow down.
7. You are enough now. If you have to repeat this to yourself every day, do so. Begin to repair the way white supremacy and capitalism have wrecked your self-esteem and self-worth.
8. Understand exhaustion is not productive. You are not resting to gain energy to be more productive and to do more.
9. Listen more.
10. Create systems of community care.

What does resting look like in practice? The list on the next page has been shared by hundreds of thousands of people on our social media as a meme. It touches a place inside us that is looking for a clear way and a daily guide. It is important that those drawn to the message of rest have a flexible path, supplemented by our own experimentation and imagination. You are the expert of your body. Your body knows more than we give it space to share. Our body is its own technology. Reimagining rest is about more than naps. It's an ethos of slowing down, connecting, and reimagining. The practice of rest is the way forward. The work of The Nap Ministry starts and ends with the power of people experiencing in their bodies what intentional, connected rest feels like. There are not enough words to explain to anyone what deep, tender rest feels like. Rest must be practiced daily until it becomes our foundation.

Resting can look like:

1. Closing your eyes for ten minutes.
2. A longer shower in silence.
3. Meditating on the couch for twenty minutes.
4. Daydreaming by staring out of a window.
5. Sipping warm tea before bed in the dark.
6. Slow dancing with yourself to slow music.
7. Experiencing a Sound Bath or other sound healing.
8. A Sun Salutation.
9. A twenty-minute timed nap.
10. Praying.
11. Crafting a small altar for your home.
12. A long, warm bath.
13. Taking regular breaks from social media.
14. Not immediately responding to texts and emails.
15. Deep listening to a full music album.

16. A meditative walk in nature.
17. Knitting, crocheting, sewing, and quilting.
18. Playing a musical instrument.
19. Deep eye contact.
20. Laughing intensely.

Rest simplified my life. It made things possible that felt impossible before. Deciding to push back against a violent system by taking to my bed solidified that I could do anything and further demystified the lies of grind culture. Fear and scarcity are a big part of how the culture keeps us bound up in the hamster wheel. Our own personal experiences and the continued reinforcement we receive from those around us paralyze us with disbelief. I was told repeatedly by employers, friends, teachers, politicians, and church leaders that life was for doing, hustling, and following a path to wealth and accomplishment. I have heard, "The early bird gets the worm," "I will sleep when I am dead," "If you don't get up and get it every day, nothing will ever work for you," "While y'all sleep, I grind," "Burn the midnight oil to get things done," "Team No Sleep," "Rise and grind," and "Pull yourself up by your bootstraps." All these toxic sayings and more are a part of the language of a culture determined to increase production and profit.

I keep hearing about the ways we exhaust ourselves to be seen as valuable and I am wondering when we will shift to see our inherent worth. When this happens, we will be closer to liberation. How can we access pleasure, joy, and liberation if we are too tired to experience it? This is a central question of the Ministry. An inquiry to process and constantly examine. We speak so highly of all the material and nonmaterial things we desire to feel whole and expansive without addressing the sleep deprivation, exhaustion, and disconnection we suffer from. What will we be able to access and identify when we have aligned with our goals and dreams? I think about all the times busyness and exhaustion have stolen my joy and possible life-giving connections. How many times have you attempted to connect with a friend or loved one but a brutal work schedule and a pull to hustle more have severed the connection, stolen your time together, or made it almost impossible to bond? How many parents are missing out on their children's activities and memories because of the call of a sixty-hour workweek or multiple jobs? Grind culture harms the community by making it normal to work and go to bed exhausted and get up and work more. The urgent wheel of capitalism spins on unconcerned with those existing in it. Capitalism commodifies whatever it can and doesn't allow space for us to experience the full spectrum of being human.

Along with stealing your imagination and time, grind culture has stolen the ability for pleasure, hobbies, leisure, and experimentation. We are caught up in a never-ending cycle of going and doing. Growing up and well into my adulthood I was taught that hobbies are for side hustles to make extra money. Leisure and vacations were a thing of rarity. From my birth until I was twenty years old I never went on a family vacation or saw my parents go on vacation. Poverty made this almost impossible as every penny coming into the home was used for bills and daily expenses. When my dad did have personal time off and vacation time from work, it was spent running errands, catching up on appointments, doing repairs around the house, or spending time doing more work at the church. My first time going on vacation came when I flew to California to see my uncle Dennis while away at university getting my undergraduate degree. Our time to explore, wander, figure things out, and decompress were few to none. The idea of living a full and simple life is complicated by the complexities and inequalities of our toxic culture. This demand to make space for time to just be is crucial to our healing and liberation. We will not make it without it. The amount of connected and intentional rest we can embody becomes a lifeboat on a raging sea. It pours into our capacity to allow for the act of care and love to save us.

We must uncover, simplify, and let go of our addiction to busyness.

Let our rest be a resurrection. Let the veils be lifted so we can feel, see, taste, and smell the power of our rested selves. May we realize a full mental shift must be made to reimagine and reclaim rest as holy. May we be excited by the impossible and move through any cynicism or hopelessness to emerge on the other side steady with love, persistence, and hope. Rest can save, sustain, and prop us up when we feel weak and our backs are against the wall. Our greatest hope to thrive and disrupt is to rest deeply and intentionally. The rest is the work. It is how the portal for liberation and a reckoning will emerge and remain open. May the portal of rest be our refuge. May we go there often.

PART TWO

DREAM!

To my Ancestors: your labor and the theft of your body will not be in vain. I will rest for you. I will recapture the DreamSpace you lost. We will be resurrected together there.

Inspired by: Daydreaming, Octavia Butler,
Audre Lorde, Womanist Theology

It would be smart for us to not
Turn our backs on rest and care
We cannot afford
to be exhausted and disconnected!
We do the work for them when we
Are afraid of our own power.

A DAYDREAMING MOMENT I EXPERIENCED WHILE GRIEVING:

As my eyes closed, I began to imagine my braids rising to become propellers that would allow me to levitate and fly away to another planet. This planet has never experienced racism, sexism, classism, or any type of hate. People sleep up to eighteen hours a day like cats. During the sleep time, their dreams produce all the labor they need to survive and thrive. The food is grown via dreams. The planet is a sanctuary for Black bodies that have been destroyed on Earth via violence and oppression. Those people are now on the council that serve as the spiritual advisers to the entire planet. Trayvon Martin is there, Rekia Boyd is there, Sandra Bland is there, George Floyd is there, and Breonna Taylor is there. They are all together, wearing white while smiling and resting.

This vision came to me in a thirty-minute daydreaming session. It soothed me and allowed a quiet space to grieve and rest. It allowed me to feel in my body and mind an alternative to what has been done. I call my daydreaming *brain love*. This Ministry uplifts daydreaming as one of the many forms of rest. A form of rest that can be accessed at any time. A mini-nap. As a child, many of us were punished for daydreaming while in classrooms. The teachers, trained under grind culture, assumed daydreaming was a student not paying attention. We slowly learn our time to imagine and download new information is wrong and not a part of learning. We begin the lifelong process of disconnecting from our bodies and learn to ignore the subtle and bold ways that our bodies and Spirits are communicating with us constantly.

I can daydream for hours a day and vividly remember this as a daily practice since I was a child. In those daydreaming moments, I was processing my own history and imagining worlds that felt real. I was creating history as I paused and let my mind and body connect. I have always been living in between time as an artist and a creative. I remember being seven years old and sitting on the cement porch of my two-bedroom childhood home in Harvey, Illinois. I will never forget this porch: smooth cement, with four steps that expanded into a stage area, big enough for a chair and surrounded by an intricate iron design. I would spend entire summers sitting on the stairs and staring at the sky, singing to myself, creating stories, bird-watching, and holding space for my mind to wander.

As I got older, these moments happened less and less. I was rushed off by my parents, teachers, classmates, colleagues, managers, and friends. All of culture is in collaboration for us not to rest. There is no system in our culture that supports and make space for us to rest. This culture does not want you rested unless it is attached to your increased labor and productivity. No one will give you rest. This is an outlier investigation. A counternarrative. It is trust work. It is healing work. It is decolonizing work. It is a subculture holding space for the blossoming of a resistance.

> A metaphysical space. A key component of this rest movement. This is the preparation, the request, the alternative, the counternarrative, the free fall.

An alternative community of those curious about rest must be uplifted and seen as a possibility. In Octavia Butler's *Parable of the Sower,* the young main character serves as inspiration for our dreaming: "I'm learning to fly, to levitate myself. No one is teaching me. I'm just learning on my own, little by little, dream lesson by dream lesson."[1] This idea of a dream lesson resonates so eloquently as motivation for beginning the unraveling and healing process. The truth that we may be afraid or unsure of how and when we will rest is valid. We can move through our guilt, shame, and fear that will emerge from reclaiming our bodies and time as our own. This is a vulnerable truth that we should not run from or hide. It can be overwhelming to go against the dominant culture's desires and plans. We have been taught to hustle, fake it till we make it, ignore our bodies' cues for rest, all because our systems have been created to ignore and push the laborers and the workers as hard as possible to increase profit.

The "Dream" aspect of our rest work is deeply tied to the metaphysical and spiritual. It is a time to be free from the confines of linear and grounded reality. The idea of being trapped in the box of "the practical" must be suspended during your deprogramming. Grind culture thrives on us remaining in our heads, unable to allow the technology of our divine bodies to soar and develop. There is massive knowledge and wisdom lying dormant in our exhausted and weary bodies and hearts. I believe the dreaming part of our unraveling will be the most challenging because it goes against all we have been socialized to maintain the pace and disconnection of grind culture. White supremacy thinking has taught us there is only a binary and the rigidity of this type of thinking keeps us available to the toxic systems, but unable to inhabit the divinity of our true selves. This is a time to simply stop and feel. A time to not force or attempt to make sense of what can and will happen when we allow our bodies to heal from the massive load we have been carrying consciously and unconsciously. Can you remember a moment in your life when you have been told that the machine pace of your days is not normal? Sit with this for a moment. Breathe this in for a moment now. There has been no space for any of us to dream of anything outside of what we have been born into. To hear the simple and bold proclamation "You are doing too much. You can rest. You can just be. You can be" is revolutionary. To believe it and continue to dream up ways to feel and find rest, care, and healing is liberation.

When we recognize this, we can, little by little, begin to honor our bodies and trust our ability to learn new ways of being. We don't have to be burned out, sleep-deprived, painfully exhausted, or disconnected from ourselves and each other. Even when we don't have all the answers for the best ways to deprogram from our brainwashing regarding rest, we can still go forth. We can always be open to dreaming into the process of rest. For many, rest is not a familiar proposition. It can be unsettling to experience the unknown ways rest can save you. We must continue to learn, trust, and experiment. If we lose hope, we must take to our beds and dream ways to find motivation again.

To rest in a DreamSpace is a red brick through the glass window of capitalism. I want our intentional rest to scream at oppression on a bullhorn, then emerge soft and full. Slowly whispering in a pace that feels unnecessarily slow and awkward until it becomes your heartbeat. Let the space that dreaming asks for channel you back to your true self. The tender human being bound up by a violent duty to overwork to justify your worth. The dreaming is our work. The resting is our goal.

There has been a DreamSpace theft. Our ability to dream, pause, and daydream has been replaced with the robbing of time, self-worth, self-esteem, hope, and connection to ourselves and each other. By putting people to sleep we are waking them up. How do we dream about a future we want to see? How do we simply tap into our dreaming flow? Who taught you the capacity to dream? Who are the sharpeners of your vision? When did your desire to daydream fade away? When did you begin to confuse the idea of daydreaming as frivolous and a waste of time? How can you begin to welcome yourself into a DreamSpace that is waiting for you to tap into? How can you begin to disconnect from the lies of grind culture enough to fall into a moment of dreaming? It will take courage to deprogram yourself from the brainwashing of capitalism. It will take hours and hours of daydreaming and silence to maintain an energetic flow that will be a guide for your liberation.

Womanist theologian Emilie Townes beautifully shares the fullness of liberation as a process. In her article "Ethics as an Art of Doing the Work Our Souls Must Have" that appears in the anthology *Womanist Theological Ethics: A Reader,* she speaks about how distinct liberation and freedom are: "An important distinction must be made: liberation and freedom are not the same. Liberation is a process. Freedom is a temporary state of being. Liberation is dynamic. It never ends."[2]

Reading her work was the first time I began to rest in the beauty of liberation being a lifelong practice. This ultimately gave me the permission and vision to take up to dreaming.

There was time now to just be. Before experiencing this revelation, I believed that I had to figure out everything in my internal and external life that was causing me harm and correct it immediately with the information I had in front of me. Things were always urgent and rushed. A feeling of anxiety of what needed to be done was always hovering over me. I was never taught that I had a wealth of healing information and guidance waiting for me in a slowed-down state of a DreamSpace. I was told the opposite: that you had to always be doing labor to fix. I didn't see my body as a place of infinite wisdom but instead saw it as a tool to be used to push, create, figure out, and do. Most of us surviving the demands of grind culture are here. I know this by how so many react when they first hear of our work and they begin to sink into the idea that it's about way more than actual naps.

Daydreaming is a form of rest and feels like the opening of your heart doing what it's supposed to do. It feels like my granny's soft arms while she rubs my head. A blanket of care swaddling you tightly. A comforting now. We are socialized into systems that cause us to conform and believe our worth is connected to how much we can produce. Our constant labor becomes a prison that allows us to be disembodied. We become easy for the systems to manipulate, disconnected from our power as divine beings and hopeless. We forget how to dream. This is how grind culture continues. We internalize the lies and in turn become agents of an unsustainable way of living. Remember, grind culture is not some pie-in-the-sky monster away from us. It is in our everyday behaviors, our lack of boundaries for ourselves and each other, the choices we make, and how we engage with ourselves and our community. We are grind culture. We must rest and dream.

Audre Lorde is the inspiration for our dreams and our dreaming. I tell everyone that follows this Ministry to read all of her work. Immerse yourself in it. Rest with it. Let her radical ways of thinking hold you like your lover's hands. Take time with reading, processing, and healing. It is not a race. Urgency is a myth that preys upon your fears about the future. Like Audre Lorde, I am totally enamored and lay my body on the altar of poetry. I am a dreamer because I am a poet. In her essay "Poetry Is Not a Luxury," she poetically shares her attachment and belief in poetry as necessity for hope. I sometimes lay down and read her poetry with the hope that I will fall asleep while reading it, so I can drift off to sleep floating on her words. Each stanza taking me deeper into a dream state. "Poetry is not only dream and vision: it is the skeleton architecture of our lives. It lays the foundation for a future of change, a bridge across our fears of what has never been before."[3]

I don't believe I would have arrived on this journey of dreaming if I was not a lover of poetry and a poet. I sometimes wonder if I would have been able to hold space for the possibility of shifting culture via naps. Maybe I could have made it to this point without the collaboration of art but it would have been a harder climb. For me, poetry, like rest, comes from the silent place of our listening. Poetry, like rest, opens up corners of the unknown while guiding effortlessly. Poetry makes sense of meaning and allows us to put things back together that have been torn apart. Poetry, like rest, can be scary to engage with because of the mystery it allows for, but this is exactly why we must face our fear and dream and let rest guide our healing and curiosity.

Rest is real-life conversations.
I don't know any other way
to go.
Rest is the road map.
The guiding force—a truth teller.
Rest is a meeting with self.
With a typed agenda.
Rest is on your knees whispering words silently,
on the right side of the bed.
Rest is lunchtime dreaming.
The energy of the Rastafarian who showed me how to
pray standing up,
with my eyes open
hands stretched wide.
"Because how will you see and know when prayers are
answered?"

Rest is holy oil
from my mama's wooden dresser.
Pompeian Olive Oil, the fancy kind in glass.
Blessed by the Elders.
Poured over our heads as we rebuke the devil.
Rest is the laying on of hands.
A force field all around you.
Rest is a dream made real.
A portal.
An honest place.
A trusting place.
A sacred refuge.
A dissertation-length longing.
Rest works.
Rest dreams.
Infinite power moving.
Care surrounding us.
Rest is a gift and an antenna.
An ancient call dangling on the tips of tongues,
from a head lightly connected on a silk pillow.
Rest is holding us close.
Rest is home.

Once I decided that I would rest and dream, no matter the consequences, when I took a "let the chips fall where they may" approach, ease, support, and clarity came quickly and easily. Radical faith is what grounds my life ethos and therefore it grounds how I study rest. Possessing extreme faith is a practice in living on the edge yet feeling tucked in and protected. Once you settle into it, you gain power from the feeling. You become magic. You can soar. You can dream.

I am hopeful that this Ministry is disturbing the idea that blinds us to the possibilities waiting for us on the other side of exhaustion. The more I have personally experimented with rest, the more I have been cracked open and expanded into what is truly possible. I have observed rest bring me back to myself in a way that feels natural and deeply connected. For close to ten years, I can consciously remember moving through life in a daze. The more we rest, the more we will wake up. If rest provided survival and held us during enslavement, during a time when our bodies were owned and families separated, why do we limit what it can do for us now? Why do we box it up and smother its resurrecting flames now? If rest is truly liberating, magical, and all-powerful, how dare we limit it by the lies of white supremacy, capitalism, patriarchy, and ableism? I think we are living beneath our potential as divine beings with a body ready for freedom. I know that radical rest will save us if we let it. I know that allowing your mind the space to feel and daydream will change things.

For Black people who are descendants of enslaved Africans via the Transatlantic Slave Trade and chattel slavery, consider the fact that your Ancestors built this entire nation for free with their stolen labor. Use this knowledge to tap into what they have already done, so you don't have to grind yourself into oblivion now. Your Ancestors want to make space for your ease and rest. You must stop long enough to receive this insight in your dreams and downloads. I believe in the portal of resting; there are answers waiting for us there.

History is so important to the foundation of The Nap Ministry. Our remembering of history is nurtured by daydreaming. I am actively inspired by the justice work of the 1960s and, since I was a teenager, was obsessed with studying the history of the Civil Rights Movement, Kingian Nonviolence, Rosa Parks, and the scholarship of Malcolm X. While these paper mentors—people you learn, gain inspiration from, and exchange ideas in a relationship centered on studying their writings—people I never meet in person, offer great inspiration, my ability to embrace mystery, history, Spirit, and dreaming came from my grandma Ora. My family history shows up right alongside the curriculum I studied in school. Along with her modeling what it can look like to reimagine rest when I was a child, the way she lived her life and thrived is a master class in surrendering to a DreamSpace. She is an Ancestor but regularly shows up in my dreams now. As a young girl, she would tell me that I was her favorite in between our gardening sessions and philosophical conversations on the plastic-covered couch in her small living room. I would sit underneath her wide arms and listen as she spoke in what seemed like another language of mystery and wonderment. We connected on a spiritual level, and I was attached to her like glue. To me she knew everything, had home remedies for every ailment, cooked large pans of blueberry cobbler, opened her home to any and every family member who needed a place to rest their head. But, it was watching her daydream, rest her eyes, pray, and prophesize about the ways of Spirit that drew me into this world of embodiment and dreaming and kept me locked in. She once told me I should never be afraid of the dead when we were driving past a cemetery on our way to the corner store. She said: "I ain't scared of dead people. I'd sleep in a graveyard peacefully. Spirits are all around us. I am more worried about the ones walking upright on Earth. These are the ones you got to watch out for. Keep your eyes on the living." The directive to "keep my eyes on the living" has crafted a path for my curiosity to grow. I am totally focused on the ways in which we as a collective can save ourselves by resting. How can we dream ourselves free?

My dreaming and daydreaming are forms of rest. We don't have to grind. It is disconnected and violent to do so. Dreaming creates energy, allows me to connect with my deepest ideas and offers space. Space to just be and to become free from the demands of a fast-moving, nonstop culture is so important. Without it, we will remain caught up in the endless cycle of trauma that grind culture creates. Grind culture keeps us all in a cycle of trauma; rest disrupts this. I daydream daily and have used this rest practice when there was no time to stop, lay under a blanket, and rest for a full sleep cycle. It is a part of the meticulous love practice. Our collective dreaming is the next dimension in this work. We must continue to stay in the DreamSpace.

To stay in a DreamSpace requires practice and vision. It requires opening up to the beauty of time belonging to the people. How can we reclaim the space we have to dream?

Techniques to create space to dream:

- Cultivate deep community that is not allowed to post online. Find and create spaces of intimacy, accountability, and vulnerability.
- Be subversive like my Ancestors on the Underground Railroad, like my Ancestors during the Great Migration. Invent a space of joy, freedom, and rest right now. Right in front of you. Lay down.
- Wander until you get lost. Be like the maroons. Decide you will never be enslaved. You are not on the run since you don't belong to the systems. There is nothing to run from.
- Rest by slowing down. Rest in secret. Rest out in the open. Get off these phones. Write more handwritten letters. Document your existence in real time offline.

- Barter and participate in mutual aid, make community care your biggest goal, learn to grow your own food, or support a Black or Indigenous farmer who does, build with an herbalist and other root workers.
- Rest as if your life depends on it, no matter what, regardless. This is how we will thrive.

The spiritual dimension of rest is evident at our Collective Napping Experiences. The room is lovingly and carefully curated for the portal of rest to open and hold us. The elements for these experiences have remained the same since the first one back in 2017: yoga mats, pillows, blankets, candles, a rest altar containing archival photos of Black people resting, raw cotton, jars of water, fresh flowers, and a soundtrack of curated rest music. The first event was to be a one-night-only art presentation. A chance for me to curate all the knowledge I was learning in graduate school and an opportunity to bring together the archival research that guided the formation of The Nap Ministry. I expected maybe ten people to attend. In the end, forty people came out to sit and nap at the rest altar. I didn't know most of the forty in attendance. They all came to rest after hearing about it in small, local newspapers or from a friend. They were soothed by a soundscape of nature while cuddled up on floor pillows, wrapped in blankets I collected from my own home and my mama's house. As I walked around slowly connecting with the room, there was a moment when everyone in the room was peacefully sleeping at the same time. A powerful silence engulfed the room and I remember being overwhelmed by this divine moment, as forty strangers shared space in such an intimate and vulnerable way. Everything felt so sacred, safe, and expansive as the energy of collective rest filled the room. It opened my eyes to how honored I am to be trusted with guiding people into a dream state.

After two hours of people going in and out of the portal of rest, I had to wake people up so the room could be uninstalled in time for the next event that was booked later. They could have slept for the entire night. So many tears emerged when I held space for the "Nap Talk" after the rest experience. The tears always happen at every Collective Napping Experience, whether in person or virtual. People wake up crying from the realization of how exhausted they are. They didn't realize how intense their burnout was until experiencing a nap in the middle of the day. This moment of pause offered so much insight. Others cry because they are overcome with emotion that they rested without guilt or shame for the first time in their lives. At a Collective Napping Experience hosted at a public library in Atlanta, a woman shared with the group that she is usually lonely and, in this moment of rest with others, she felt held and seen. As I was packing up to leave, a rester approached me and asked when the next one was scheduled. In her words, "There must be more of this. I need it."

I had never planned on doing more regularly. But folks kept asking for the next one and I remained open to the creative ways the rest experiences could be installed with the community. I never said no in the beginning to any request to install a rest experience. This has been a beautifully expansive experience that has allowed for the community to rest in yoga studios, church basements, city parks, conference rooms, libraries, theaters, bookstores, gymnasiums, public schools, universities, art galleries, homes, apartments, and shared workspaces. Wherever there is a clean floor or outdoor space, there is the possibility for a rest experience to be installed and curated. During that first rest experience, I looked across the room and thought to myself how special, sacred, liberating, and anointed collective rest feels.

From our first signature program, the Collective Napping Experience has continued to evolve from 40, to sometimes only 2 people, and to virtual rest events with several hundred on the call. One of the most beautiful napping experiences I have facilitated occurred in the mountains of Colorado for a retreat called Stress Protest, hosted by the organization Girl Trek. More than five hundred Black women from all over the country came together for a weeklong experience of workshops, classes, and fellowship. Fifty

Black women gathered into a large gymnasium filled with yoga mats, pillows, low lighting, and a curated playlist of Black healing music. Their ages ranged from twenty-one to sixty-five years old. They were ready and excited to lay down together. As everyone settled in, I watched bodies go from tense and controlled to relaxed and open. For thirty-five minutes the entire room was held in a state of fluid and free rest. The air inside felt hopeful and full. Silence was given the reverence it deserves as the breathing of all in the room began to sync up and take each person into a concentrated and deep slumber. I slowly walked around the perimeter of the room with a lavender incense in my hand. The trail of smoke rose gracefully behind me as I quietly observed what it means to disrupt and push back. The power of fifty Black women slowing down for an hour in the middle of the day to just be without any labor requests, phones, or worries. A soft space to land. During the Nap Talk a rester shared a dream that happened during her nap about her grandmother who recently passed away. They spent a connected moment together in her dreams. She was visibly emotional about this visit and found it healing and comforting.

At each nap experience, I read The Nap Ministry invocation as an open invitation to rest. Right at the moment before an individual drifts off into a dream state, while between the awake and sleep worlds, I begin slowly and softly with the opening line, "The doors of the nap temple are open." I continue passing through each stanza carefully as this rest call leads the willing into the portal of rest. In the middle of the manifesto, there is a line of gratitude. Slowly and with intention I read over the bodies of everyone stretched on the floor, "Thank you for living. Thank you for resting. Thank you for resisting." After the reading concludes, half of the room is usually already in a rest state, with the other half on the way. For forty minutes the soundtrack plays, and we wait for the spirit of rest to show up. It always does. Rest has never failed us. Dreaming will never fail us.

In the beginning, I wasn't sure if people would be able to nap in a room, during the middle of the day with strangers, as a woman they are not very familiar with, calling herself the Nap Bishop, offers a pillow and blanket. Would someone leave their purse and cell phone, take off their shoes and cuddle up under a freshly washed blanket and matching pillow in a room full of people unknown? Will they feel comfortable? How deep will the sleep be? How will they react when it's time to wake up? It sounds so far-fetched and unrealistic, and this is why it works and has landed in the hearts of so many all over the country and the world. The Nap Ministry has always been the personal experiment of an exhausted and curious Black woman artist. I was aware of what rest had done for me, but to watch it transform into a collective healing moment for others has been a complete blessing.

Many of our early experimentations were held at Yellow

Mat Yoga and Wellness in Atlanta, Georgia, one of the few Black-owned yoga spaces in the city. So many magical and powerful moments have happened there: Someone told me while they were sleeping, they felt the floor shift and felt swaddled in a blanket. It felt so real that upon waking she asked me if I had walked over to her to place a blanket carefully on her. I said no because I never touch anyone without their consent and while they are sleeping. I simply sit, walk around, observe, and hold space for the room to transform. I am in protective receiving and quiet mode. She was shocked that her dream felt so real it made her believe I tucked her in. During a Nap Talk group exchange, a woman started weeping loudly. I asked if she wanted to share the root of the emotion and she confessed that she has never had anyone say "thank you for living" to her. She went on to say that for weeks she has been depressed and feeling unworthy. Being able to feel gratitude for her life via the words of a poem and a dream while sleeping awakened her to peace and a moment of lightness.

I wake people up with care by either adjusting the light or playing a song from the curated playlist starting with the volume low and slowly increasing. It gives time for people to come out of a rested state very gently. There is no rush. There is no urgency. The Collective Napping Experiences allow for moments to simply be, to receive care, to experience leisure, to daydream, to dream, to not be on a clock, to not feel rushed and to be adored simply for being and not for what we have done. As the music comes up, eyes begin to open, limbs begin to stretch, and blankets begin to shift. This is a moment of embodiment and a time when connections can be created. We connect with the deepest parts of ourselves when we are rested. This is also a moment of intimacy and vulnerability. As we prepare ourselves to deal with the harshness of everyday living, rest becomes a space of physical and spiritual softness. An antidote to the hidden rage present in an exhausted body. Rest is a protest. Rest is a beautiful interruption in a world without a pause button.

Dreaming is the way we move toward liberation because it is a direct disturbance to the collective reality of life under capitalism. Grind culture is violence. This can't be stated enough and we must repeat it over and over to ourselves as we deepen into this truth. You will read it throughout this manifesto. Grind culture is violence and violence creates trauma. We have been traumatized deeply. Our divinity as human beings have been ignored and degraded. Thousands of people privately come into our social media inboxes monthly and courageously share the deep guilt and shame that they feel about resting. "I feel like I should be doing something," "I feel worthless when I am not checking off things on my to-do list," "I feel lazy and unworthy if I have a day full of leisure." Bound up in guilt and shame, unable to settle into the gift given to us when we can just be. This is where the dreaming begins. You are activating all the power that has been forgotten. You are making a new path.

There are no rigid guidelines on how to begin embracing the beauty of dreaming. The beauty of this work is in its inherent flexibility and call to experiment. It's a deep trust that you must grant yourself. It is a leaping. A trust practice. A divine activation. The experimentation began to take shape with my exhausted body reading the book *Slave Testimony: Two Centuries of Letters, Speeches, Interviews, and Autobiographies* for a research paper for a graduate class on Cultural Trauma. I have owned the book for close to twenty years and it sits on my bookshelf as a reminder of history. I take it off periodically and read through chunks of it at a time. I was always shaken by the first-person account from the enslaved. This peek into their world. A window into and document of the micro-histories of their lives. At 750 pages, it is not a book to read in one sitting, instead a reference guide and archive. The book is "the first systematic attempt to compile in one volume several different kinds of slave sources. It includes 11 letters written by slaves between 1736 and 1864, 8 speeches, 129 interviews conducted by journalists, scholars, and government officials between 1827 and 1938, and 13 autobiographies appearing in periodicals and rare books between 1828 and 1878."[4] The Nap Ministry would not exist without my engagement with this book. Many nights, I laid on the couch reading and falling asleep with it on my chest. I was hypnotized and calmed by these voices. I spent hours with colorful Post-it Notes marking pages in categories of land, work life, religion, pain, and family. I was attempting to get a deeper vision of what their lives were like. Hoping to latch on to a word or phrase that would open another meaning. I deeply wanted to communicate, and as my curiosity built it turned into rage as I became obsessed with the details of the work life entries. As I slept and napped daily, sometimes passing out after a fifteen-hour day of work, school, internship, and studying, I begin to dream about my Ancestors and what their bodies went through. This rest experimentation started here.

I remember one day in 2013 when I was in my first year of graduate school. I was in a fluid state of exhaustion and constant movement. I can look back on it now and name the deep sense of disconnection I was experiencing. It felt normal to be exhausted, tired with fifteen-hour days of studying, classes, work, and mothering. This is just the way it was. I accepted there was no time for a moment of rest. When I finally passed out at night, I don't even remember if my rest was fulfilling and I definitely didn't remember any of my dreams. I looked at my calendar the first day of school as I handwrote my daily schedule into a planner:

5:30 a.m.—Wake up to study a little and start breakfast for my son.

6:30 a.m.—Wake up my son so he could get dressed and make it to bus stop by 7:30. (Why are young children going to school so early? More evidence of grind culture being headquartered in public schools.)

7:30 a.m.—Walk to public bus stop to take bus to train station less than two miles from my house. (Sometimes I would walk.)

8:00 a.m.—Take train for thirty-five minutes to first stop.

8:40 a.m.—Transfer to bus that goes directly to campus.

9:00 a.m.—Arrive to school and start first class.

10:00 a.m.—Start second class.

11:00 a.m.–12:30 p.m.—Study.

12:30 p.m.—Lunch.

2:00 p.m.—Start third class.

3:00 p.m.—Work-study job in archive library.

6:00 p.m.—Study and writing time in library.

9:00 p.m.—Start journey back home.

9:30–11:30 p.m.: Public transportation consists of three buses and one train. After rush hour ends around 8:00 p.m., the system in Atlanta slows down the frequency of schedule, so it takes longer to travel.

Midnight—Arrive home, shower, eat a snack, go to bed, start over.

Start back over at 6:00 a.m.

I look at this schedule now and can't believe I kept this up for so long without a full breakdown physically or mentally. This is a standard day and most times it would be more packed hours with a required internship done on Saturday and Sunday.

I name academia as one of the main sites of grind culture. The headquarters of pushing through exhaustion, competition, expectations, and a lack of balance. During the final exam season, I watched people live in the library never once leaving, bringing sleeping bags to lay under tables and in between the bookshelves. I spent numerous times living in the library for overnight group study sessions with classmates during finals week. The stress, anxiety, overloaded curriculum, and pressure we normalize in public schools and higher education are toxic and dangerous for everyone involved, but particularly toxic for young children and young adults who are still developing a sense of self. They are exposed to the lie that their worth is determined by how much they can accomplish constantly and it's reaffirmed and rewarded when they push their bodies to the limit to do well in classes. Many also begin to pour themselves into the life of perfectionism, which is a function of white supremacy. We internalize the toxic messages received from the culture and begin to hate ourselves unless we are accomplishing a task. We seek external validation from a violent system void of love. Dreaming and creating the space to dream is the remedy and cure.

The energy of love is central to community care. Dreaming becomes the prescription and balm needed to sustain this rest resistance long term. Loving ourselves and each other deepens our disruption of the dominant systems. They want us unwell, fearful, exhausted, and without deep self-love because you are easier to manipulate when you are distracted by what is not real or true.

To deepen into the reality of how deeply distracted and disconnected we are from the ancient truths of rest, we created Resurrect Rest School in January 2020 as an ode to the Freedom Schools of the 1960s. The school is an alternative and temporary space of deep study, community care, and commitment to education as a key to our freedom. With this in mind, our Resurrect Rest School was formed to uplift the need for targeted education around the principles of the Rest Is Resistance framework. It was created to deepen into the practice of why collective dreaming is necessary. It is a push-back to the quickly consumed, shallow exposure on social media that many believe to be the end all to their education and unraveling from capitalism. During the Rest School we study, analyze, and discuss text together. Around a table with highlighters and pens we dream up new ideas and ground ourselves in communal time to just be. We pass out copies of liberation text for everyone around the table to engage and analyze. There are herbal teas, healthy snacks, fellowship, and it all ends with a collective nap. The

Resurrect Rest School differs slightly from our Collective Napping Experiences because it centers on intensive study and makes space for us to test out our learnings and to question. The school allows space to deepen into the theories that hold this work together. To shift culture and truly transform, as it will take study and a consistent effort rooted in visiting a DreamSpace often. It's a process of learning and unlearning. It's a process of love. The text "Love as the Practice of Freedom" by bell hooks was assigned as the first study experience. I recommend all to read it and meditate on how she is pushing us to think in new ways about the true power of love in justice work. She writes: "Without love, our efforts to liberate ourselves and our world community from oppression and exploitation are doomed. As long as we refuse to address fully the place of love in struggles for liberation, we will not be able to create a culture of conversion where there is a mass turning away from an ethic of domination."[5]

To dream, to rest, to turn away from the toxicity of grind culture are radical acts of love for ourselves and our culture. I often speak about how naps will not save you if you are still upholding anti-Blackness, white supremacy, ableism, and patriarchy. All these things are the opposite of love and care. We can't continue to attempt to dream up new ways of being while still supporting systems of domination. We can't simply talk about the hopes of a world centered in justice while we continue to exhaust ourselves and each other and remain in allegiance with grind culture. Our dreaming must center on love, community care, and the courage to go deep into cracks of what the training of white supremacy and capitalism has taught us about who we are and what belongs to us simply because we are alive. Until we grasp on to the truth of dreaming as a path to resistance, we will remain caught up in a space of shallow and self-centered thinking. We need dreaming to free us.

I want to reread the words of bell hooks over and over again and let them sink deep into the reservoirs of my heart. Her poignant revelation about our motivation to move against domination and injustice only when it directly affects us and we feel pain shook me to the core and confirmed the ways in which individualism is a path to death and destruction. This ethic of love is the basis for all movements dedicated to social change. Love is the path. I believe rest is also the path. Community care and less self-centered longings will elevate the idea of rest as resistance so that it remains a spiritual and political practice.

Rest is somatic work—connecting your body and mind. Rest is anything that slows you down enough to connect with your body and mind. It is an ethos that holds firm to the body as a site of liberation. Active rest is also valuable rest. In active rest your body can move, swim, walk, dance, and tap into a portal. Since the beginning of my imaginings around what rest is and can be, I have repeated constantly, "This is about more than naps." This work is decolonizing and culture shifting. We are speaking about actual napping: laying your tired body down on a surface, closing your eyes, and sleeping for a shorter time than a full sleep cycle. But we are also speaking about the mystery of what is not seen by the naked eye and instead felt energetically and spiritually. You must experience rest. The praxis is rest. You will have to rest to believe in this message. You won't be able to skip steps and rush the dreaming that it will take to be liberated from grind culture. This is why I love rest as a liberation practice. It gets to the heart of the matter.

When you are exhausted, you lack clarity and the ability to see deeply. Your intuition and imagination are stifled by a culture of overworking and disconnection. You must be open to go deep into the cracks to examine and to understand. It may take years to fully crack open and it will be a lifetime of practice, care, and creativity. It's your life, body, and community; therefore, it is yours to hold, protect, love, and care for. Exhaustion will not save us and will only lead us further into the clutches of grind culture. Rest is shapeshifting and wants to hold our hands as we usher in a well-rested world. It's about more than naps and is a full-on pushback and political statement against the systems that want to see us constantly moving, doing, and going in a frenzy. When we tap into the power of our bodies, we understand that our bodies are a miracle, a legacy and a place of extreme power. The foundation for love and reclamation.

I know there are many who have misunderstood the totality of our message of rest. I am learning by observing the patterns that have emerged on our social media accounts over the years. Many have purposely ignored the social justice and political thread that runs through. It can be easier to believe resting is simply about retiring to your bed when you are tired instead of beginning the messy process of deconstructing your own beliefs and behaviors that are aligned with white supremacy and capitalism. You must be committed to studying how training under the abusive teachings of dominant culture has you bound and limited. This is healing work. This is justice work. When we are aligned against the ideas of the oppressive culture, we understand we didn't arrive on Earth to be a tool for a capitalist system. It is not our divine purpose. You were not just born to center your entire existence on work and labor. You were born to heal, to grow, to be of service to yourself and community, to practice, to experiment, to create, to have space, to dream, and to connect.

Our rest is a living document and work that will be endless and fortified by our dreaming time. It is embodied and must remain there. Let the message never be co-opted by anyone attempting to erase its origins away from the spiritual, political, and justice message it resides in. Let words elude us for the sake of obtaining the language in our DreamSpace. We have lost our way and are seeking a reorientation that upholds rest and care. Let our bodies be their own GPS devices leading us to our natural state. A state of rest and connection. A state of love, dreaming, and accountability. A state of wonder and curiosity to what is available to us on the other side of exhaustion.

I want us to understand that nuance is freeing and freedom. There is no such thing as cookie-cutter healing. Everyone brings with them an origin story, a history, and identities that are interconnected. There is room to rest in the freedom of managing your own deprogramming journey. It is never either/or and always both/and. You don't have to grind, hustle, accept burnout as normal, and be in a constant state of exhaustion and sleep deprivation. You don't have to kill yourself spiritually or physically to live a fruitful life. This connection work is about restoring, remembering, reimagining, reclaiming, reparations, and redemption. Learning to make a way out of no way and seeing to the other side of trauma. It is believing you are worthy of rest because you are alive. Our bodies and souls want to be well, to heal, to be rested, and to be free from the hold productivity has over our lives. We are worthy now of rest, care, and space. We are worthy now of living in a place that respects our bodies for what they are: a divine dwelling. Capitalism wants you to be a machine. You are not a machine. You are a divine human being. We can put ourselves into a rest and care trance in our quiet moments. We can evoke the power of the tongue as another tool in our protest kit.

More Love.
More Care.
More Therapy.
More Dreams.
More Daydreaming.
More DreamSpace.
More Meditation.
More Love.
More Calls to Say, "How Are You Feeling?"
More Love Letters.
More Bedtime Stories.
More Strength to Love.
More Naps.
More Rest.
More Sleep.
More Care.
Place Us in a Dream Trance.

Softness is available to us. Care is available to us. Rest is available to us. Intimacy is available to us. Community is available to us. Sleep is available to us. Justice is available to us. Pleasure is available to us. I call myself an escape artist as an ode to those before me who found a way to subvert systems to gain autonomy, agency, and justice. I view my imagining and crafting of The Nap Ministry as my ultimate escape. The work of this Ministry is a perfect cocktail of my thirty years as a poet, artist, activist, scholar, researcher, dreamer, and truth-teller. To be an escape artist is a remembrance and nod of respect to my Ancestors who floated along the paths they created on the Underground Railroad, during Jim Crow terror and the Great Migration, always claiming survival and freedom as the goal. I want to float down the path to rest. I don't want a seat at the table of the oppressor. I want a blanket and pillow down by the ocean. I want to rest. I dream of a well-rested world outside of the toxic systems in place now. I am so grateful to them for placing their bodies on the altar of rest during times of turmoil and joy.

This is not a book offering a step-by-step rigid list for you to find rest in a capitalist system. As a culture, we have already given ourselves over to the rigid binary that is neither expansive nor imaginative. We've done that and been tricked and manipulated by grind culture to falsely engage with living on a timeline that is geared to production always. We don't need more of the same boxed-in and limited thinking. It's time to tap into our imagination. It's time to go deep into the cracks of who we are as humans to be able to make sense of our world. Capitalism is new and our bodies are ancient. Grind culture has created a bunch of exhausted, disconnected, and traumatized people moving through life, unable to tap into their true power. We need rest to connect back to ourselves and dream. We will rest!

PART THREE

RESIST!

"When the human body is the locus of domination it can also be the focus of resistance."

—*Dr. Carol Newsom, Apocalyptic Imagination Class Lecture, Emory University, 2016*

"It is only when people live in an environment in which they are not required to exert supreme effort into just keeping alive that they seem to be able to select ends besides those of mere physical survival."

—*Howard Thurman*

Inspired by: American Maroons, Somatics, Third Spaces

Why we resist

The idea of resistance is central to the message of rest and to our life as human beings. I talk a lot about the ways in which the brainwashing and socialization of grind culture begins when we are born and sometimes even before, in the case of the birth of my son. We are always resisting in invisible and blatant ways. Our soul has very likely already been resisting the ways in which grind culture abuses and pushes us while degrading our divinity. I believe we resist because our souls are calling us to see differently. Our souls are our center. An invisible, clear quiet force that is required for living. It knows the way, just like rest. So, when we are not caring for our souls or even acknowledging that we have one, we are not able to possess the inner knowing we are born with. Rest is soul care because rest deliberately pays close attention to the deepest parts of you. Rest places soul care at the center of our wellness and liberation. None of us will get free without resisting toxic systems that blind us to the truth of who and what we are. We should be curious about our souls and the ways rest can comfort, heal, and uncover what grind culture has never allowed us to feel. Our bodies have information to share with us. Our souls are foundational to us and to our resistance journey toward rest. The soul, while being foundational to how we navigate life, has also been a mystery to theologians and religious leaders throughout history. Many have claimed that the soul is the center of who we are and the most beautiful and powerful part of your body. What is your soul saying? Is your soul already resisting the terror of grind culture quietly and unconsciously? Is the idea of rest as a form of resistance appealing to you because it touches you in a way that is beyond comprehension? Have you had moments of observing the pace of your life and it didn't feel true to your soul? I believe our souls are saying to us that it is a travesty to not rest and without the care that rest provides our souls die. This is why we resist outwardly and inwardly. Why we must resist and listen to the faint sound of our souls guiding us to see our world more rested and more human.

Detective of my own soul
Lover of the unknown
Believer in ghosts
I don't find them scary
Always resisting because our souls are deep
The veil is thin
Rest a veil buster
I ask my soul:

"Give me sight to see what is really happening.
Give me a third eye. A heart eye."
There is always more to the story
There is always more to the lie
Depending on who is doing the telling
I'm concerned with the harsh realities
Our brutal orientation toward forgetting:
"We are born to rest. We are born to resist."
The unknown stories
The pieces left out
The care of souls
Reclaiming our divine right to rest

The resistance part of our "Rest Is Resistance" framework is what drives this work toward a political and social justice movement. It exists in the long-standing Black liberation tradition of a politics of refusal, maroonage, and outlier connection. When I think of resistance, I envision all the small and large ways my Ancestors and family remixed and reimagined their lives in a toxic, anti-Black world. The way they went deep into the cracks to create spaces of joy and freedom. Tricksters using their own intelligence, intellect, and creativity to make a way out of no way. To make a way that was and is disinterested in the ways of this world, so the crafting of a new way became a daily ritual.

As I've said, this is about more than naps. It is about a deep journey toward decolonizing and returning to our natural state before the terror and the lies were given to us. To resist means to soften into the powerful proposal of thriving right now. Of not waiting for permission from a toxic culture that blocks justice and moves from a spiritually deficient place.

The idea of rest as resistance has always resided in me but I deepen into it the more I spend time listening to my soul while deeply daydreaming about the Underground Railroad and being inspired by the maroons of North America. Harriet Tubman is one of the many muses for this work. An enslaved woman focused on the choice of freedom or death. Her inner knowing that life was on the other side of the trauma of being enslaved. Harriet Tubman crafted space to listen, to strategize, and to pray while guiding people on the Underground Railroad. She stopped to listen to nature, to track the sounds of owls, and she was deeply in tune with the stars and her spiritual world. I like to envision that she was never caught by police while on her freedom journey because she paused, listened, and prayed. Her subversive and deep refusal to be in bondage is the energy I'm holding on to. This energy of refusal and maroonage grounds my personal experimentation with rest as resistance and is a North Star for this Ministry. Resistance is a rich, spiritual posture. It opens the possibility for reinvention and connection. To know that we are divine and cared for can allow us to refuse the lies of any oppressive system. To declare to the systems, "No, you can't have me. My body belongs to me. I will never donate my body to grind culture. I will rest," is a bold political statement against a system that has used bodies as a tool for oppression for centuries. Our focus is to lay down because it is our divine right to do so, not because it will prepare our bodies to be more productive. Our rest movement is not focused on productivity. It is instead a political and social justice movement rooted in our collective rest. We must resist together. We must liberate together. We must rest together.

We are going up against such violent systems in our attempt to disrupt and push back: white supremacy, capitalism, ableism, patriarchy, classism, anti-Blackness, homophobia, etc. Any system that degrades and ignores our divine right to have care, rest, leisure, and space must be examined and illuminated. The time is up for any shallow wellness work that doesn't speak about dismantling the systems that are making us unwell. We must blame and interrogate the systems. They are the problem.

A hidden history that is not well known by most in our culture is the story of the American maroons. This history has been foundational to my understanding of resistance when I begin connecting the dots between rest and liberation. The maroons were Black people navigating the terror of chattel slavery by refusing to be a part of it. For close to two centuries, they leaped off slave ships as they pulled up to the shores of North America to never be seen again, they organized and left plantations for the caves and deep woods of the South, they created their own communities outside of the slavery, and they were not fugitives and instead, living in a Third Space, a temporary place of joy and freedom. They liberated themselves and each other in community. Existing in two worlds. Being in the world of chattel slavery, but not of it. They claimed their autonomy and sovereignty while the violent system of plantation labor raged around them. They told the systems, "No, you cannot have me. I don't belong to you," and they embodied this call intensely. I first learned about the American maroons in 2014 while attending a weeklong training in New Orleans for organizers focused on Black land liberation. The fact that I was in my forties, a lifelong scholar of American history, and in graduate school studying Black liberation and had not yet heard of this powerful history before this training must not be overlooked. There are so many stories that have been hidden, erased, and lost. Americans know very little about their own history and even less about world history. We are moving through life exhausted, disconnected, and out of touch from who we are, where we come from, and the implications of this today. Truly knowing the extreme details of history has the potential to open up a large well of possibilities, motivation, blueprints, guidance, and inspiration.

When I say I have tapped into the idea of reimagining rest while in a capitalist system, it is because I am inspired by the power of the American maroons. If there is required reading for this Ministry, I would easily say it's the book *Slavery's Exiles: The Story of the American Maroons* by Sylviane A. Diouf. The book is an intensive resource for the ways of resistance. The way maroons organized themselves to survive and thrive is breathtaking. The way they created a whole world within an oppressive one to test out their freedom and regain autonomy reminds me of the spiritual and metaphysical ways we must reimagine and shape-shift our way to intentional rest.

It took months for me to begin to wrap my mind around what the maroons were creating and crafting. They were not runaways, and instead they simply never accepted the role of enslavement and never allowed the plantation to be home. It directly relates to the ways in which I began viewing myself as I continually unravel from grind culture. If we are to find rest right now, while capitalism rages on as a global force, we will have to view ourselves from a different lens. Things will be different. We must act different. We will make choices differently. We will have the opportunity to resist differently and to imagine alternative ways of resting.

We must make space for others to rest, remaining committed to what is true. Despite the terror of grind culture, we rest. We recline, curate, and create moments of rest wherever we can. We must remain committed to reclaiming our divine right to rest and participate in community care.

We must spiritually disconnect from the shenanigans of grind culture while physically still living in it. A metaphysical and spiritual refusal must be developed deep within. Capitalism may not fall in our lifetimes, and it is not redeemable, so the work is to begin to reclaim your body and time in ways that seem impossible to imagine. We must imagine. The time to rest and resist is now. We cannot afford to wait for the powers that be to create space for us to have moments of deep rest and care. If we wait, we will forever be caught up in the daily grind. To resist now means we will have to decide on rest as a reimagined way of life. Like the maroons of the American South, my rest practice begins with the mental, emotional, and spiritual gifts I discovered being stolen from me via grind culture. I inched closer and closer to the edge and as my exhaustion increased my Spirit started whispering, "No more. You must slow down. Rest a little." I listened.

I want to offer to your deprogramming process that you carefully begin to embrace the space of resisting the lies of dominant culture. It is a holy place. It is a creative, inventive, innovative, expansive, and transformative space. So much is possible here. Instead of fearing the unknown of what's on the other side of slowing down, begin to see it as a sacred place that is ready to hold and make space for your gifts and inherent talents. Grind culture has placed fear as our only compass and keeps us frozen in a way that is now a habit. To start and continue the process of resting in our toxic and urgent culture, our imagination must be our only compass. It is the glue that will hold you together as you give love to yourself via rest. Imagine a life outside of grind culture right now. You can create it because you are more powerful than you believe. We are more powerful than we believe. What liberation can you craft outside of grind culture? What information can you exchange with yourself and others to find rest? Are you ready to begin slowly by imagining what it would feel like to have everything you need? Are you curious enough to try rest?

My rest practice started off with fifteen-minute catnaps on campus in seminary and once I arrived back home. I also rested when I was attempting to study. I implemented sky gazing moments in between classes that involved sitting down outside and staring at the sky. To be in nature, breathing slowly, while I was sometimes navigating my day on four hours of sleep from the night before was life shifting. When I couldn't go outside, I would stare out of windows and watch the leaves on my favorite tree sway in the wind. When a window wasn't available, I did techniques I learned in ballet class, somatics training, and breathing exercises I learned in childbirth workshops. All three practices involve extreme focus, intentional breathing, and coordination.

A senior student paired with me as a mentor shared this wisdom: I would have a very difficult time in a theology program if I didn't find ways to get out of my head and into my body.

As an artist, this would also be key to my success. During my time in seminary, I enrolled in dance and somatics classes as an opportunity to balance out all the heavy brain lifting happening from studying and reading seven days a week. I discovered that as a graduate student in the theology school I could petition to take classes in any of the other schools so I ran directly to the dance and theater department and began taking a ballet class with undergraduate dance majors. This experience heightened my understanding of what the body holds and is capable of. To dance three days a week on barre while a live pianist played our cues transformed me and offered a quiet solace that felt like an anchor in a raging storm. While learning the fundamentals of ballet posture, we built up to spotting to complete a turn. With my head in place, I would pick an eye-level visual object on the wall in the dance studio. Most times it was a small black dot, maybe a speck of paint, that stood out immediately. Week after week, I turned my eyes to it and dialed my focus inward. The act of tuning in calmed me immediately. After a semester of this practice, my body was training itself to float and turn. A challenging process of listening and surrendering. "You will not be able to complete the turn without going inward and connecting your mind and body," the ballet instructor would say consistently. As my eyes burned into the wall, I began to rotate my body until my eyes reached a rotation and fixation that transitioned into my head quickly rotating, taking my body with it as I returned to the same spot of my start. The turning is such a metaphor for a resistance practice rooted in rest. To resist the notions of grind culture we must remain locked into the silence and power of a rested body.

The fixation on the visual object to facilitate a turn. The head quickly rotating to overtake the body to return. The connection from your brain to your core to your feet to begin and end a turn all provided radical mechanics capable of translating to the ways to find rest. I found comfort in knowing a turn, a shift, and a leap were within my reach simply by connecting and tuning in. The connection to your body is a spiritual experience. I have never felt closer to the Creator than when I am completely lost and found in the creative process of embodied art making. To be able to defy gravity and turn 360 degrees on one leg takes extreme focus, trust, and surrender. Knowing that rest is always possible is revolutionary for my soul. It also takes a deep level of surrendering to the power of our bodies and souls. Will you trust yourself to turn inward toward rest?

So when I couldn't find the comfort of a bed because I still had six more hours left in an already long day, I turned inward and fixated on my breathing and visualized my body at rest.

To turn your attention inward and away from that which is causing trauma, even for a few minutes consistently over time, is liberating rest. It's a mind shift and a collaboration with your body and mind, centering on repairing the harm that never stopping and pushing through creates. Grind culture requires that we ignore anything that is not centered on labor and doing. To resist while living in the very system pushing a machine-level pace will be a slow and meticulous action.

The illusion of living within grind culture offers the myth of control. Many of us are on automated, robot, machine mode and there is not room here for the magic of mystery and Spirit to move in your life. As we ignore our body's call to slow down, we disregard the inherent wisdom that is granted to us by being alive. We can figure things out. We believe that we haven't been scammed and manipulated since birth on the ways of white supremacy and capitalism. We must give thanks for the evidence of this systematic brainwashing. Once you see it, you can't unsee and I want you to see with clarity and focus that we are all living in a place that makes us unwell mentally and physically. We all have pieces of this sickness in us in some way. We have been bamboozled. This is why it's so critical that we create systems of care to help people dismantle and decolonize their minds. None of the way we are living under capitalism is normal. I want you to feel this in the widest parts of your heart. You are not unworthy. The systems are unworthy. Who were you before the terror of oppressive systems making you believe lies about yourself and about your fellow human beings? What have you been told about your worth and existence? How do you make space to transcend the confines of grind culture? How do we make space? How do we make a home? How do we build the world we want to live in? How can we be subversive and flexible? How do we craft a resistance that feels like home?

Resistance is a spiritual practice and a practical map. We learn how to make a way by building as we go. We resist by crafting ease and invention. We resist by reclaiming autonomy and leisure. We remain flexible and ready to shapeshift as our bodies call out for rest. My offering to you as a main point of how to resist always goes back to the brilliance of the maroons of North America. Living and thriving within two worlds, they built safe spaces. Crafted an alternative place of freedom miles away from the plantations and sometimes right in its backyard in the deep bush, hidden in plain sight while tucked away.

"Maroons also lived in caverns. They were a natural refuge that offered more space and better protection than trees, as Josh of Richmond County, Georgia, found out. He first tried to live under a hollow trunk, but when a bear got the same idea, he had to find other accommodations: large caverns bordered his owner's plantation and Josh appropriated one. George Womble of Valley, Georgia, knew a couple who stayed in a cavern near their plantation and raised their children there. Their cover was so good and they were so successful at eluding capture that they only reappeared after the Civil War."[1]

How can you resist the constant pull of grind culture in your daily life? Are there moments of laser-focused connection you can give to connect your body and mind? Can you slow down more? Can you do less?

How do we resist the violent systems that are embedded into our entire culture? How do we actually rest? We do it by reimagination. We do it slowly with radical faith and a constant experimentation centered in resistance.

Because we are intimately aware of the engine driving a capitalist system, our guiding forces are resistance, imagination, reimagination, invention, flexibility, and subversion. Reimagining rest looks like so many things. The possibilities are endless and infinite. Rest looks like tapping in and listening to what your body and soul want. It's extra time while bathing, even an extra ten minutes of concentrated silence. Rest is taking a leisurely walk and dancing. Rest is a tea ritual allowing you to meditate while breathing in each warm sip. Rest is not returning an email immediately and maintaining healthy boundaries. Rest is honoring the boundaries of those you engage with. Rejecting urgency. Rest is detoxing from social media. Rest is listening and healing from individual trauma. Rest is journaling so you can be a witness to your own inner knowing without the energy of others. Rest uplifts and boosts our Spirit, allowing us to know that we are enough, and the care of our souls deserves a role in our healing plans.

There is a dream and vision space that is accessible during naps. When we don't nap, we miss out on precious creative time to hope and imagine. Hope is what will sustain us. Sleep will restore us. Peace of mind will elevate us to our highest form while spiritually protecting us from the invasion of the spiritual death that comes from sleep deprivation, exhaustion, and the trauma of burnout. We must collectively continuously stress the importance of an inner peace that comes from listening to your body's need to rest and slow down. This is where our spiritual knowing resides and why we must resist anything that removes us from the listening. We must lovingly train our souls to resist the urgent pace of our toxic world, we must keep finding our way back to ourselves over and over again.

The foundation for resistance lies in our ability to

connect, listen, and repair what has been done to us due to grinding ourselves like a human machine. Our collective rest is a meditation and disruption of the violence of capitalism. Capitalism deserves to be resisted and disrupted. It is a violent, global force that constantly steals our time and power. It is not redeemable and has always been a demonic force pushing divine bodies to the edge.

My continued examination of the book *Slave Testimony* left an intense imprint on how I view my own body's cues to rest. It also highlighted the ways in which I was repeating the violence that capitalism inflicted upon my Ancestors during slavery. The book was and is a witness and mirror for me. While studying the text, I learned that enslaved people worked twenty hours a day in the blazing sun. The reports of working from 4 a.m. until midnight, every day is unimaginable and earth-shattering to me. I live in Georgia, the Deep South, and the land here holds a legacy of plantations and terror. The weather in the summers is brutal and heartbreaking. I remember once sitting outside on a hot summer day, barely able to breathe and thinking about the brutality of working for twenty hours straight in this level of heat every day. My throat became tight as tears rolled down my face imagining my Ancestors bearing this madness. To learn that my Ancestors' bodies were pushed to a machine-level pace of production, as plantation owners experimented with what a human body could sustain, is a grief I will probably hold forever in my heart and in my body. As a Black woman who has endured pregnancy and childbirth, I zoned in on the account of what the life of a pregnant enslaved women was like. I learned they worked in the fields until they gave birth; many gave birth in the fields also. To visualize a pregnant woman participating in plantation labor while nine months pregnant and then birthing in that same field left me dizzy with confusion and disbelief. This brutal reality should shake anyone to their core. This recalling stops me dead in my tracks anytime I feel the pushing of my own body to levels of extreme overworking, and it supports my commitment to rest as a form of resistance and protest. I simply cannot and will not do it any longer. I have connected the dots spiritually and physically between this history and my life today. I will resist and I will rest no matter what.

The following interview was recorded in 1855 by an abolitionist and journalist. He interviewed over one hundred formerly enslaved people. This is an excerpt from the interview with Harry McMillian. He was born in Georgia and was enslaved in South Carolina. He worked as a field hand on the plantation. These first-hand accounts guide my intentional commitment to resting, slowing down and connecting.

Question: How many hours a day did you work?
Answer: Under the old secesh times every morning till night—beginning at daylight and continuing till 5 or 6 at night.

Question: But you stopped for your meals?
Answer: You had to get your victuals standing at your hoe; you cooked it overnight yourself or else an old woman was assigned to cook for all the hands, and she or your children brought the food to the field.

Question: You never sat down and took your food together as a family?
Answer: No sir, never had time for it.[2]

When you don't see a lot of life (rest), death (grinding) becomes the alternative.

Using rest to correct what I've experienced as a Black woman in America. Engaging with rest to build the world I want to see. I want to see a rested world that is deeply connected to our divinity and not to the violence of capitalism and white supremacy. This Ministry is guided by the deep beauty of Black resistance, Black scholarship, Black history, Black leadership, maroonage, and crafting systems of care outside the dominant culture.

I've been uplifting a politics of refusal from the beginning of my experiments of what rest could do for my survival. A call to refuse grind culture. To create temporary spaces of rest and space no matter what. It's truly a deep mental mind shift to thrive in a place with no pause button. It's a Third Space and a spiritual place. It's intuitively knowing the pace is not sustainable and a politics of refusal that opens once you tap in. It's not easy since all of culture is working in collaboration for this grind. The resistance is very personal and internal.

White supremacy and capitalism have stripped us from connecting in the spiritual and intuitive realm. We have been socialized to believe in individualism and from it the false reality that everything must be done right now. To keep up with this pace, we increase and do more when Spirit work is about knowing that work has already been done for us by our Ancestors. We can tap into this portal via rest. Our human eyes and a disconnected exhausted body will never get us to the new world we are hoping to build. How can we imagine a liberated world from a burned-out, quick-paced, exhausted state? It's not possible, and that's the scam of it all.

How can we imagine a world without police if we are unable to imagine a world that includes rest for all? How can we build systems of care if we don't even care for our own bodies and the bodies of others?

Rest is a meticulous love practice. It is a correction to our bodies from the violence of living in a capitalist, white supremacist system. It is a radical love for yourself and others in a place that views your body as simply a tool for it to use and own. I believe we don't belong to these systems. I am guided with evidence from my own family and Ancestors. Rest and a DreamSpace as a place to plan and a place to sleep, rest, and invent. Rest makes invention and imagination accessible. Rest gives us the ability to test our freedom. Our souls are calling to see differently. To move differently. To feel differently. To rest. Rest as a subversive act. The deepest act of resistance.

Do not let your lack of money and possessions make you feel negative about your worth as a human being. Do not let your credit score, man-made poverty, and/or racism define your extreme power. Your body is a site of liberation. Rest in your true power. Your birth was not a coincidence. Your coming to Earth is a divine occurrence. They will tell you differently. It will be your life's lesson to fight for your life to not listen to them. You are so much more. You can rest. You can shift. You can heal. You can resist. You can lay down right now. If you are in a safe space that would allow for you to lay down, please do so as you read. If it's not safe to recline, just slow down your breathing. Visualize your favorite place to slumber and relax. Go there in your mind. May these rest moments multiply as you integrate more into your daily practice.

A politics of refusal is an ancient tactic. I cannot stress enough the importance of viewing this idea and the entire experimentation of The Nap Ministry as an ancient practice. It is not new or a trend. It is a necessity and a way of survival for many. It comes from a place of connection and knowing. My deprogramming from grind culture has taught me that my entire life is a resistance.

How to prepare your spirit and body for a nap.

STARTING POINTS TO JUMP-START YOUR CURIOSITY AND EXPERIMENTATION:

1. We cannot wait for the perfect space or opportunity to rest. Rest now. In *Part One: Rest!,* I share the need for seeing rest as not an extra treat that we must run to but more of a lifelong, consistent, and meticulous love practice. We must snatch rest.
2. We must believe we are worthy of rest. We don't have to earn it. It is our birthright. It is one of our most ancient and primal needs.
3. Our bodies are a site of liberation; therefore, wherever our bodies are, we can embody rest. This second tenet of The Nap Ministry is a mantra and a meditation.

4. Productivity should not look like exhaustion. The concept of laziness is a tool of the oppressor. A large part of your unraveling from capitalism will include becoming less attached to the idea of productivity and more committed to the idea of rest as a portal to just be. Your early understanding of "productivity" is most likely tainted by the toxic socialization we all received growing up. It must be examined.
5. Deprogramming our minds and hearts from our toxic brainwashing around naps and rest will increase our ability to craft a rest practice. Our slumber and opportunities for community care will be deeper because of our work in this area. Go slow and realize you have been brainwashed by a system that attaches your inherent worth to how much you can labor and produce.
6. Grind culture is violence. Resist participating in it. This must be flexible so please also resist the desire to become rigid. I have gone months consistently experimenting with a rest practice daily or weekly. The next week I am caught up in an all-nighter to finish a deadline. We are moving in and out of worlds all the time so give beautiful grace to yourself. Start again on rest. Keep going back to rest. Stay in the DreamSpace.

Ideas to dream into:

Every surface where you feel safe is the best place to nap. I have napped outdoors, on couches, at yoga studios, in church, on public transportation, on planes, in my car on lunch hour. If we are to embody rest while disrupting grind culture, there are no limits to where and how we rest.

Silence is a sound. Sound can be healing but it doesn't have to be from music tracks. Find and cultivate silence.

Baths. Go to the water. Salt and essential oil soaks are ancient wisdom for our bodies and facilitate amazing naps.

Stretching, expanding, and softness. Soft pillows, soft blankets, soft breathing, and a soft heart.

Detox from social media and phones regularly. This will take planning and consideration because the addiction to both is real on many levels. When I begin the process, I take all the social media apps off my phone. I also plan for open time that will emerge when I am not spending hours a day scrolling. It must be replaced with intentional rest, opportunities to connect, moments of studying, journaling, and daydreaming. You will be pulled back to your phones in a way that feels habitual and unstoppable. This is part of the process. Start with a plan of detoxing for a day and then move up from there.

Experiment with nap rituals and rest habits that work for you. Craft your rest practice.

Read poetry before you nap or write rest meditations to yourself. Designate a journal to serve as a rest journal. Repeat these meditations often.

What Rest Is Resistance is not:

We are resting not to do more and to come back stronger and more productive for a capitalist system. Rest is not a luxury or a privilege. This lie has been drilled into our brains and minds forever and it's time to begin to remove this veil. The deepest movement of your deprogramming pilgrimage will be unraveling from this false belief. One day I hope we can all deprogram from the lie that rest, silence, and pausing is a luxury and privilege. It is not! The systems manipulated you to believe it is true. The systems have been lying and guiding us all blindly to urgent and unsustainable fantasies. We have replaced our inherent self-esteem with toxic productivity. When we finally realize that a long checklist of to-do's will not replace a deep understanding of our enoughness, we will start the unlearning and unraveling process. You don't have to always be creating, doing, and contributing to the world. Your birth grants you rest and leisure as well.

Capitalism, at some point, has captured me and most of my family, close friends, and community. We are under the spell of chasing the bag, getting a coin, and hustling proudly for wealth. Hustling and grinding trying to get to the unreachable finish line of wealth that most have never enjoyed. The nightmare of capitalism has always been out of our reach; we exist only as a product of it. Keep unraveling. Give thanks for the beauty of awareness and self-reflection. Our resistance is deep healing work. There is a mirror waiting for us to look into. There is a bed waiting for us to get into.

Rest is not popular, supported, or modeled in this culture. It is an outlier movement until capitalism and white supremacy are dismantled. Therefore, we cannot wait until we are told it's okay to rest. No one will tell you this. You will have to make space for yourself and others around you to rest. Resting is not a state of inactivity or a waste of time. Rest is a generative space. When you are resting your body, it is in its most connected state. Your organs are regenerating. Your brain is processing new information. You are connecting with a spiritual practice. You are honoring your body. You are being present. All these things are so foundational for liberation and healing to take root. Your bodies don't belong to capitalism, to white supremacy, or to the patriarchy. Your body is a divine temple and a place of generative imagination. A place of healing and freedom.

I believe any work that is rooted in wellness and justice and doesn't include the collective, without a framework about dismantling and decolonizing, is incomplete work. It's work that is more of the same. To get this new world, we must tap into our imagination, our DreamSpace, and our dream lessons. I'm really interested in imagination work and things being invented. Honoring the imagination of those before us. I'm not interested in the regurgitation of what's happening on social media around rest. I'm interested in deep, slow study, research, and personal experimentation.

To date, I've spent close to ten years experimenting and researching about rest as a healing tool and disruption to capitalism. The work is still evolving. Years of me being caught up in the grind machine, pushing my body and then resting. Being pulled in and out of the fluid reality of living in a world that sees rest as frivolous. I'm interested in always honoring and referring to my Ancestors, because my resting is in reverence to them. I remain curious about what's happening in art circles, faith-based places, spiritual circles, community-organizing meetings, and in the quiet moments in people's homes, when they are offline in a non-documented moment of care and deep rest. I'm less interested in the repetitive and curated world of social media. I believe we would be closer to our rest goals if we weren't always connected by technology.

What is dynamic about the message of rest is it will be

constantly evolving and changing, as we hold space for the ways in which we can dismantle and disrupt white supremacy and capitalism. It cannot and should not be placed in a box. It is not a one-step ideal, and it will be always evolving as we grow and begin to pull ourselves deeper out of grind culture. The end is a well-rested future. Our resistance is the balm for a deeply traumatized world.

PART FOUR

IMAGINE!

"Imagination is one of the most powerful modes of resistance that oppressed and exploited folks can do and use."

—*bell hooks*

Inspired by: Afrofuturism, Harriet Tubman

Take up space.
Be risky in your observations.
Be a maroon.
Decide you ain't ever going back to enslavement.
Take a nap to receive a Word from your Ancestors.
Be subversive.
Embrace radical love that is outside the confines of tradition.
Be suspicious of everything they taught you.
Carry a research notebook.
Be curious.
Resist.
Rest.

Imagination as a liberation tool

I am not the first to trust imagination as a tool for liberation. I am forever inspired by bell hooks and Octavia Butler for believing in and teaching us about imagination as a tool of our greatest liberation. There aren't enough pages or words for me to uplift what their scholarship and commitment to telling the truth has done for my life and this rest calling.

They have relentlessly spoken about the idea of seeing and crafting the world we want to see. This part of our rest pilgrimage calls for invention and practical action. It is deep embodiment with an understanding that we must be ready to make life-changing decisions, establish boundaries, and reimagine the ways we heal. I believe this crafting includes our rest. I spend countless hours daydreaming about what our bodies and minds will be able to figure out and embody from a rested state.

I believe specifically that my Ancestors, those enslaved on plantations, had their DreamSpace stolen. A theft. The space to just be replaced with racial terror and violent labor. I like to imagine them plotting and organizing even deeper plans for freedom and maroonage from a rested state. I am astonished at what my Ancestors were able to accomplish and create from an exhausted and sleep-deprived state. I place it in the category of divine miracle, and it creates a deep spaciousness for my hope about the future. I wonder about what our bodies can do in this dimension and this time from a rested and imaginative space. What could we heal? What could we figure out? How would our justice work look different if all involved were not sleep-deprived? What transmissions could we receive in our dreams that can guide us to liberation? What insight could our Ancestors provide when we connect with them in our dreams? What revelations are we missing out on because we are navigating our life from a machine-like pace? How could your imagination be cultivated if you gave yourself even ten minutes of daydreaming daily? We must reimagine what rest is and what it can be for us. Everything that we have ever learned about rest has been false. It has been a lie. Our call is to find ways to integrate rest and to listen to our bodies. We can nap and find ways outside of napping to tap into all the ways our bodies and minds can connect and slow down. This is rest. There is rest for the weary. For those working two or three jobs and still unable to pay rent consistently. For those parenting, working, and going to school, there is rest available to you. For the body that is unable to labor the long hours grind culture requires, rest is a refuge to you. So, when I hear the responses "I could never rest," "I wish I could. I am so busy," "I feel guilty when I rest. I feel like I should be doing something," I am not overlooking the blatant reality of poverty, low wages, late-stage capitalism, corporations generating billions of dollars while the worker isn't offered a living wage and all other trickery and abuse that make it feel impossible to thrive. We understand the seriousness that exists when speaking about the life-or-death situation poverty has placed in our laps.

Rest disrupts and makes space for invention, imagination, and restoration. Rest is an imagination tool because it makes space to simply be. To be a human being is an ancient miracle that we overlook when we work so hard to prove our worth via exhaustion. If nothing else in this book resonates with you or breaks deep into the cracks of your consciousness, please let it be this: You are enough right now simply because you are alive! You are divine, no matter what capitalism or white supremacy has trained you to believe.

Imagine what it would feel like, taste like, and smell like to believe you don't have to prove who you are by your accomplishments and labor. This is at the core of this work and the foundation of imagining a new way. The culture we live under does not point you toward this deep truth. It instead has told you and reinforced the idea that you came into the world to be a machine, to accomplish, to labor, and to do. Nothing can be further from the truth and when you slowly begin to believe and understand your inherent worth, rest becomes possible in many ways.

As you begin pondering the ways you can integrate and shift your mindset around rest, naps, and slowing down, ask yourself the following questions. You can journal with them. Meditate and dream with them. Use them as a discernment device ready to guide:

1. What do I feel called to do?
2. How can I create space for me and my community to heal? What needs healing in me?
3. Can the idea of unplugging and resting for a whole month be reimagined by creating smaller moments daily, weekly?

4. What does intentional rest and care look like to you? Sketch and map out a visual.
5. How is your heart?
6. Who are you being?
7. What are you holding?
8. What story are you telling yourself? What is a more liberating story you can tell?
9. How can you create rest in this moment?
10. Are you ready to change?

I've experimented with the realms of possibility for invention by resting relentlessly and creating month-long Sabbaths from social media and labor. I have done this consistently and name it as one of the main ways I am able to continue to be inspired as an artist and activist in the midst of the beast of capitalism. What I have discovered has created space for me to be an antenna for infinite ideas and downloads. A container waiting to soak up what is already inside me while making space for the healing energy of silence. This is rest.

My Sabbath is a personal, spiritual, and political practice. I stop to declare that there is enough, and I have done enough. How would we navigate our lives if we believed deeply that there is enough? I believe the Earth is also in a state of extreme exhaustion. Capitalism is not only wrecking our lives and Spirits daily but also killing the planet itself.

The Earth needs to rest and all its inhabitants deserve a re-imagined Sabbath.

My Sabbath in November 2019 revealed so much to me about the ways in which we are existing in a numb state of disconnection that leaves very little space for community care and imagination.

Before my month-long Sabbath in November 2019, I announced and prepared for three months that I would be off all social media, no events, no email, no discussing The Nap Ministry work details, no bookings, and no traveling. I essentially imagined and hoped for a totally off-grid experience that included sleeping, silence, napping daily, lots of detox salt baths, reading books, not speaking about anything related to work, writing a little, spending time with friends and family, and total nesting at the house. Most of these things happened for me and there were so many moments of deep calm and connection, but it was also a beautiful battle. I learned so many things, but the most important was that people truly do not want you to rest because they have no model of what true rest looks like in a capitalist system. My clear boundaries and Sabbath time was invaded and disrespected constantly. Numerous times, I had to remind 90 percent of the people who I interacted with during my Sabbath that I was indeed on an intentional break. Folks would hear me verbally say it and then continue speaking about work and requesting things from me. It was fascinating to observe the trance and grip that grind culture has over us. I gained so much knowledge about how radical and life shifting this work is because it offers extreme clarity and a connection to intuition in truly revolutionary ways.

THINGS I CONFIRMED ON MY THIRTY-DAY SABBATH:

1. Our entire culture is addicted to social media and technology. This is leading us down the path to exhaustion. If you are not very intentional about detoxing regularly from it, I believe deep and connected rest will be impossible.
2. Truly practicing rest is a battle and liberation practice. No one wants you to deeply rest, because most people have never had the opportunity to practice it consistently, so there is no model for how to embody it.
3. There is a trend happening in speaking and writing about rest. Most of the culture is not actually resting. The trend of talking and writing about it is rooted in capitalism, toxic group think, and opportunity—both connected to grind culture and the way media consumes and extracts.
4. Dreaming and the DreamSpace is key to deprogramming from grind culture and is a profound space of healing and liberation. My dreams while detoxing from technology were vivid and detailed every single

night. I felt like I was in an alternate reality nightly. My intuition was heightened, and my ideas flowed. During a five-day period, I handwrote seventeen pages of thoughts and ideas. I researched the science of scrolling on devices and the effects of excessive screen time. I learned that our brains are changed by it over time. Early designers of social media platforms intentionally created scrolling pages as opposed to pages that have a stop and ending. In essence, this design function is allowing us to scroll for hours daily in an almost zombie-like state.

5. Every day I was resting and not rushing I felt another layer of intuition and connectedness pour over me.
6. The everyday pace of our culture is not healthy, sustainable, nor liberating. We are living and participating in violence via a machine-level pace of functioning. This toxic space has been accepted as the norm. It is not normal.
7. Anyone who goes against the pace of grind culture is living as an outlier and a risk-taker. It is warrior-style resistance to push back and disrupt this reality. I received more work-related emails, texts, and requests on this Sabbath than when I'm available and working. Even when the automated email message would inform the requester that I was away for thirty days,

most ignored it and followed up repeatedly. I found this to be fascinating.

8. My Sabbath was a restorative ritual that transformed my body and soul. I felt like my cells had an opportunity to regenerate and do their work of transmitting to a higher power.
9. I did not miss being on social media the entire time I was away. It was beautiful to be in solitude and not attacked with the thoughts, ideas, and commentary of the thousands of people online daily. My own thoughts had a chance to spread out and develop. I felt physically better, spent a lot of time face-to-face with people, and I wandered in my dreams and in my awake moments. I felt more human and began to float more.

How would we set boundaries for work and labor if we tapped into the spiritual dimensions of rest? I have experimented with three month-long Sabbaths in the last two years. All of them are a beautiful struggle and a practice in patience, boundary-setting, and mercy. I prepared by examining my calendar and setting an outline for all the tasks that I could eliminate. I began to tune in to requests being asked of me in the month I have chosen for Sabbath. It's so important to announce and make it as clear as possible to all in your spheres that you will not be available during this time.

Because our culture has no model for what it looks and feels like to stop and pause, your Sabbath is a teaching model and a guide. For me, my Sabbath is not a sabbatical because the latter assumes that it is granted by an outside entity for me to study, travel, write, or create. Creating a Sabbath is an opportunity for intense imagination work and collaboration with Spirit. We have the ability to imagine a Sabbath that is unique to us and only us. What a beautiful space of invention to listen to ways you can disconnect, even if it is for ten minutes, a weekend, thirty days, or as a gift to yourself for an anniversary or birthday. The intent of a Sabbath is to save us. The intent of rest is to save us.

As a Black woman, it is challenging to enact a true Sabbath. The myth of the Black woman being the mule of the world, the Superwoman and the one who will save everyone, has created a battle to stand in my desire for a Sabbath. The world is so addicted to the constant labor of Black women. Since the founding of this country, Black women were forced to serve in the deviant role of the mammy, a faithful, unselfish, loyal worker giving of their bodies and labor to the family of the enslaver. This being a role she adored and excelled at is a myth we still see today. This culture loves to take and receive from Black women's brilliance without any reciprocity or shame. It is accepted and expected.

I knew this intellectually, but really was able to lean into this harsh truth during times I was in Sabbath. During my first Sabbath, in which I declared I would not be taking on any labor, requests, or projects, I was asked all these things by those who knew I was on Sabbath. They would say, "I know you are on Sabbath, but are you able to spend an hour recording this podcast?" I also received constant emails that read, "I have read on your auto-reply message that you are on a Sabbath for thirty days; if you come back before the thirty days, I would love to jump on a call to discuss something I need." There is no vision or model of a Black woman to be free from the exploitation of her emotional, physical, and spiritual labor. Since our kidnapping and arrival on the shores of North America, our bodies have been a constant source of exploitation, extraction, violence, and disregard. This continues in the present as Black women make up a large part of the caregiving labor force while being paid the least of everyone else on the planet. Our intellectual labor is stolen constantly without credit or thought. We are seen as the ones to save the world while being the mules of the world.

This is why I demand and will continue to announce my Sabbath to the masses and to those I'm closely engaged with. I include a detox from social media as a part of my Sabbath because social media is labor and, as an extension of capitalism, it wants to keep you always drooling for more. We are never full as we scroll for hours, get into debates about things we know to be true, fight off internet trolls and those stealing our intellectual scholarship. The entitlement we feel to the inner workings of people's lives is satisfied by our repetitive interactions online. We are lured into the performative ways we believe will get us free.

A truth that is uncomfortable for many to hear and swallow is this: Once we have internalized capitalism and are deep into the cycle of brainwashing, we don't want to rest, we don't know how to rest, and we don't make space for others to rest. Our imagination and sense of invention no longer exist in an abundant way when we are tied up in the shackles of grind culture. I will continue to call the rest movement being guided by The Nap Ministry as imagination work because it is our greatest hope for the future.

In her essay for *Essence* magazine in 2000, "A Few Rules for Predicting the Future," Octavia Butler shares a powerful truth related to imagination: "The very act of trying to look ahead to discern possibilities is an act of hope."[1] If I could repeat this over and over like a call to prayer blasted on speakers throughout the land, stirring in my heart, whispered in ears, etched into our psyche, and tattooed gently in the palms of all who feel even a glimmer of hope, I would do so. I am struck by what it means to discern and how when you are spinning dizzy to keep up with the pace of this culture, there is very little room to see the light. We are unable to distinguish between what the systems demand from us and what our Spirit and bodies know to be true. We have to make space for daydreaming, sky gazing, for our bodies to come back to their natural states. When we are sleep-deprived, exhausted, and burned out, a cycle of trauma emerges. We can cultivate our imagination to anticipate and hope for the future.

We underestimate imagination. Belittle it as a waste of time, a thing done by frivolous children, and constantly push the false idea that imagination does nothing but allow a moment of escapism in a harsh and cruel world. We use this same perspective when we think about rest. The imagination that I am uplifting is not escapism, although I find escapism to have a powerful place, especially in the lives of oppressed people. This imagination work allows individuals to be able to see what is possible. Everything we see on Earth today, all the systems that we're living under, were created by someone. They didn't exist until people sat down and imagined a way to make sense of their world. In the case of white supremacy and capitalism, those who created and experimented with these violent systems found a way to hold firm to the toxic belief of profit over people. They found sinister ways to subjugate and commodify human beings in a way that would lead to their power and wealth.

We too have a right to build and reimagine our world. We must begin the steady process of testing our possibilities. What can a rested world look like? What could a world where capitalism doesn't exist be like? What if poverty was no longer created? What could we imagine as alternatives to the toxic individualism that is leading us to collective death? Our imagination has the power to tap into new worlds. We must fight for it. We must envision it. We must see things clearly first before they can be.

I hear the narrative a lot that it's time for institutions and governments to make it easy for us to rest and this is where the Rest Is Resistance framework differs. We are resting *regardless* of what any of these systems are doing. We are not waiting. We are not asking permission. We are driven by the spirit of being subversive, inventive, and disruptive. We know this will not be easy, but we trust our divinity, the power of collective care, and a laser focus on tapping into our imagination via rest to make a way for our unraveling from grind culture. We must always remember that we can't be aligned with white supremacy or capitalism without consequences.

There is not one way to integrate rest into our culture. It will take the power of thousands of hours of imagination time to get there. I am asked by many people to share some quick tips and fast ways to rest more. These requests come in an urgent fashion as they sit and wait for me to rattle off a concise and neat list that will allow them to unravel from a lifetime of socialization. But to understand there is no magic bullet is liberating and hopeful. It is a counternarrative to the anxiety-filled, rushed way of being we are so accustomed to.

The invitation to approach your healing via rest in thousands of ways is revolutionary. Revolutions take time. The process is long and slow and for that I am thankful.

This is not a book that you will pick up to obtain a step-by-step list and rigid system on how to find rest in a capitalist system. Our culture thrives in the myth of quick, convenience-style processing. We have done that and don't need more of the same boxed-in and limited thinking. It's time for another way. Time to tap into our imagination and return to what our bodies and Spirit already know. It's time to go deep into the cracks of who we are as humans and begin to investigate and uncover. The wisdom of your body knows. It is yours to usher out of grind culture's toxic world. Your body is in a state of extreme exhaustion and therefore can't offer you the brilliant guidance waiting for you on the other side of disconnection. Connecting with your body from a rested state will open many portals of information. You have permission to experiment. Come back to yourself. Lean in. Invent. Pause so you can make sense of our world. This is not cookie-cutter healing. Capitalism is new. Our bodies are ancient and the way to heal ourselves is ancient. Rest is ancient. This is a moment for deeper imagination work that will lead us into the deepest parts of ourselves. This is abolition. This is imagining a new way. This is dreamwork.

I don't feel a sense of dread or anxiety in my being. My

hope and joy are internal and not built upon the shenanigans of our toxic culture. I'm firmly planted in the brilliance and power of rest, community care, and of what I can imagine in collaboration with God and my Ancestors.

I'm firmly planted in imagination and the beauty of my own liberation. I'm laying down and daydreaming. I refuse to let grind culture gaslight me into despair and exhaustion. I can never forget what my Ancestors were doing even during racial terror. They centered joy, found rest, created art, and found pleasure in themselves and their families daily. This is my hope and North Star.

The Nap Ministry is a commitment to an ideal that may seem unattainable. This makes it revolutionary because it creates space to imagine and hope. Both are the keys to our liberation. We can begin to use rest as a path to cultivate our imagination. When we stop to investigate and examine all the tools we have within us to interrupt the dominant systems, the portal opens. We will have to pause to listen and hold space for slow inquiry. A rest practice will be a lifelong journey of curiosity. I am curious about the following: What does a rested future look or feel like? How can we collaborate to create a world where there is a space to rest for all? What information is available to us when we are in a rested state that we are missing? How does exhaustion work against the power of alignment and flow? What healing and ideas are our Ancestors waiting to transmit to us via our dreams?

What would happen if we could collectively imagine that we have everything we need?

I started my career off as a poet more than twenty years ago. I was writing and performing poetry in the rich spoken-word scene in Chicago in the late nineties. I also made a living teaching poetry in Chicago Public Schools and in after-school programs for community organizations with young people. My work centered on young people between the ages of six all the way through high school. One recent experience that is close to my heart and justice practice is a session that happened in 2017. I was teaching in Atlanta, Georgia, with an after-school program of young people between the ages of eleven and seventeen. I lovingly organized a beautiful curriculum on poetry writing. My goal was to introduce the concepts of details, metaphor, and colorful language. I asked them to write and map the journey of their lives from now until birth. Every week I would collaborate with them for two hours. They would read poetry from published authors like Langston Hughes, Alice Walker, and Nikki Giovanni and practice the art of performing and expressing through poetry.

About halfway through a fourteen-week program, I began to understand that I should shift the curriculum. I needed to move away from my original lesson plans and go deeper into guiding their imagination via studying Afrofuturism. I did this because every week these young people wrote about the reality of their lives, the poverty, the drug abuse, the gun violence, the voicelessness they felt as young people, the unemployment happening within their families, the prison industrial complex many had experience with. Week after week, I got these breathtakingly violent and heartbreaking poems from young people describing the horror of their lives. I was grateful for the safety they felt to share with me and their classmates and understood the importance of telling the truth of your life. There was no balance, no hope, and no invention for what could be. So, I turned to science fiction, comic books, music, and film to introduce the teachings of Sun Ra, the father of Afrofuturism, Octavia Butler, Missy Elliott, and the blockbuster movie *Black Panther* that was premiering at the same time as our residency together. I was surprised when this group of teens admitted that they didn't watch science fiction, had never seen a hard copy comic book, and had very little knowledge of the Star Wars film series. Many of them had a hard time taking themselves outside of their daily reality. This solidified my understanding of how oppression works to steal our imagination. This is particularly true for marginalized people. Black and Brown people living in communities destroyed by the created violence of poverty and injustice are constantly robbed of the space to imagine. So we began a deep dive into Afrofuturism.

In Afrofuturism, there is a future where all current

problems are solved. The future is now. Afrofuturism has implanted into me a new memory curated by my deepest desires. Black dream making and creation. The father of Afrofuturism is Sun Ra—born in 1914 in the Deep South of Birmingham, Alabama, jazz composer, pianist, and poet known for his experimental music and film. His brilliant teachings: To transport Black people away from the violence and racism of planet Earth to the creation of a Black planet. His artistic reaction to the trauma of Black life in the United States brings deep joy, hope, and expansiveness, even if just in our dreams. Black people are given the space to see beyond, above, and around their current place in a violent society. This imagination brings peace and a liberated future. Our rest work must be planted deeply in the sea of imagination. Afrofuturism is a trusted collaborator for the Rest Is Resistance framework because Sun Ra was driven by the idea of the impossible. Deprogramming from grind culture must come from a place of that which has never been done. We must fold ourselves into a reality that is far away from what we are given every day by oppressive systems. Studying Afrofuturism and the path of Sun Ra will be extremely beneficial to the crafting of a lifelong rest practice. Our DreamSpace, the portal that rest provides, and our desire to build a New World rooted in rest are supported by the time-bending philosophy of Afrofuturism.

I am struck by the call to believe that the future is now

and in the future all the problems from this world are already solved. Impossibility guided Sun Ra deeply. "In his album notes and interviews, Ra began sketching out an 'Astro-Black mythology,' a way of aligning the history of ancient Egypt with a vision of a future human exodus 'beyond the stars.'"[2] I connect Sun Ra's work to my crafting of a rest practice because in order to begin to disrupt from grind culture's theft of my time, I must believe in the impossible while guiding my own path toward leisure, softness, ease, rest, and care. I must believe that it is possible to rest. I must disconnect from the lies I have been told about my worth, even for a few minutes a day, so that it becomes truth. I must remain hyper-focused on the impossible and gain power and energy from it. My rest is possible in a white supremacist, patriarchal, capitalist system, because of my attraction to life and Spirit. We need this ethos if we are to shake loose from the stronghold grind culture has over us. We will need to dream without borders and to believe that everything is possible. We can't continue to be trapped by binary thinking. We can't continue to stay stuck in the literal, afraid to let our minds and hearts wander to the liminal space waiting for us when we dream and rest.

By the end of the after-school program, the young people were standing up reading poems describing what a Black Planet looks like for them. They spoke of a planet where you didn't need to go to public school and learn things for a test and instead you were born with all the knowledge you would need to thrive. Your breathing would activate more learning as you needed it. There was a place where guns didn't exist, and food grew freely so no one was ever hungry. Money was never invented, and you could sleep for days without anyone calling you lazy. One of my favorite students, an eleven-year-old boy, had this exchange with me: Me: "So, why do you think traditional science fiction creators depict the future without Black people present?" Youth: "Because they think we won't last that long! But they are wrong. We are the future." All I could do was smile and say, "Yes, we are."

Our resting now opens the portal for a rested future. The future is now. In the daily movements of connecting with our body, reclaiming space, and imagining collectively. The future is rest. We aren't told that it is possible to rest within a capitalist system. Our imagination is limited to even dream up the possibility of a daily nap. We may never get to a fully anti-capitalist world, but our imagination is our resistance. Imagination is a form of care. The violence of living under white supremacy and capitalism wears down our ability to dream and invent. We are easily manipulated when we are exhausted and caught up in the grind. There is power in the gospel of rest and in ministry concerned with survival, thriving, and making sense of the world. Rest is waiting to order our loves, soothe our exhausted bodies, and disrupt the trauma of navigating life at the pace of a machine. Reimagining allows for memory to blossom and gain strength. This strength can dismantle grind culture and offer redemption. We need to remember and make sense of the toxic world we are attempting to leave behind when we intentionally rest. This will disrupt the status quo and carry us into an imaginative state.

I bear witness to the ways in which grind culture has wrecked bodies, hearts, and minds. I bear witness as an act of resistance and for radical hope. I bear witness for all names of my Ancestors who were exhausted by a system that saw them as nothing more than a machine. For my great-grandmother Rhodie, with her pistol used to defend herself during Jim Crow terror. For my granny Ora who always remembered to find a way no matter what to have peace and rest when it felt impossible to others. For my daddy, Willie, who crafted space to just be before punching into a time clock. There is liberation in the remembering and in the telling. Exhaustion confines the spirit and rest empowers it. I am a survivor of the grips of capitalism and the American nightmare that is one of constant labor and fear. It is from the recalling and remembering after the trauma that many can begin to process fully how they have held and dealt with the unimaginable.

DreamSpace—How I tapped in while napping

It was not a quick process to begin tapping into the DreamSpace. I can still remember the exact moment my body and mind shifted into the unraveling process. I was laying on the couch in the living room in our small home after returning from a long day at school. It was late, around midnight, and I took out my notebook to begin reviewing notes from a lecture that day. I had a quiz the next morning, so I felt the constant pressure of academia. As I reviewed my notes, I eventually fell asleep with the notebook resting on my chest. While asleep I had a vivid dream where it felt like I was being held in a tight swaddle. It felt constricting but soft and comforting. In the dream my body felt free and rested even though in my awake world I was suffering from years of sleep deprivation and burnout. This prophetic dream was a glimpse into what my body and mind could feel like. This offering allowed me to understand that it is possible to feel soft and held in a world that feels hard and cold. It was tender and real, and I began to follow this urge and demand more moments in this portal any way I could.

Between growing up in the Black Church, watching what Spirit can do for and to a person during embodied worship, paired with my obsession with Afrofuturism, it is easy for me to connect the dots to rest as a portal for healing. I am so grateful for this upbringing that allowed me to see liberation, community care, self-love, and imagination in real time. This created a temporary space of freedom in a world that hated my Blackness and womanhood. I watched the Holy Spirit show up in the Pentecostal denomination and as a result I am very comfortable with embodiment and the idea of trusting deeply what is happening behind the scenes. Things eyes and ears can't see and hear.

My mother is a prayer warrior. It is her spiritual gift, so as a child I watched her praying on the phone with her friends and her praying for me through the phone and feeling movement happening. There is the possibility of transmuting trauma to power. Telepathically communicating. Cells changing and evolving. Rest as a generative space feels like freedom to me. We aren't told that it's possible to live a life that makes space for deep rest, care, leisure, and space. It is not only possible. It is happening and it is the foundation that will usher in a new world. We cannot continue to ignore our bodies while aligning with grind culture.

Rest on a somatic level is a small resurrection. I have always been interested in the concept of community resurrection. We all may be familiar with resurrection only from a Christian perspective with Jesus rising from the dead on the third day. Outside of a Christian lens, I believe resurrection is a powerful idea for activism and disruption. A resurrection is a waking up into a new thing. It's life, insight, breathing, refusing, thinking, and movement that is alive and made new. Rest is resurrection. A literal raising from the dead. Grind culture is a spiritual death.

Rest is medicine to project us into the future. Rest disrupts and makes space for invention.

I believe the deepest part of oppression lies in the theft of our imagination. I love when someone says, "I'm speechless. I am without words." In our culture we live in our heads always ready to theorize, analyze, and make sense out of everything. In rest and dreaming, we surrender to the unknown. We can allow a moment of freedom. We can test out what it feels like to be without the limits of capitalism. Nature's way is growth. You cannot achieve deep rest in a consistent way if we don't detox regularly from social media and the internet. Technology is not built to support our rest or make space for our rest. Social media is an extension of capitalism, and we must be constantly critiquing it for what it is doing to our bodies.

I realize that the idea of resistance can feel scary at first. Many times, I've offered resting as an alternative to grinding and the immediate response from a traumatized exhausted body is: "How will I be able to pay rent? How will I be able to eat? That sounds amazing but that's not for certain people. It sounds like a dream. It's not realistic." I am grateful to not be realistic and for the legacy of imagination and trickster energy shown to me by my Ancestors. I am grateful that Harriet Tubman was unrealistic when she decided to walk to freedom, guided by the stars, her intuition, and God.

The idea of justice being unrealistic is deeply embedded in our psyche. We've been socialized from birth to ignore our deepest imaginings, to rush and to believe that our entire lives are built upon what we do for capitalism. It is a relentless attack happening daily and hourly. Rest exists to repair this trauma, fear, and misinformation. I did not land upon this rest idea from a privileged place. When I started resting to save my life and connect with my Ancestors, I was a poor, Black, queer women in graduate school on student loans with thousands of dollars in debt. I had been unemployed and underemployed since I was a full-time student. I had a job as a student worker in the archive library on campus barely making $12 an hour for a few hours weekly. I was also working for free as part of an internship for my studies while taking a full load of classes and caring for a six-year-old child. I am and was a first-generation adult graduate student with a child and a husband who was working fifty-plus hours a week to pay our rent while I studied. Once I finished my program, I couldn't find work in my field even after going on countless interviews. I remember sitting on the side of my bed crying because I had negative $25 in my bank account, no car, and no savings. This is not a movement created by a person speaking about rest from some sort of position and privilege outside of being traumatized from capitalism and white supremacy. I am telling you it's possible because I am the poster child and witness. Rest saved my life.

This is an experimentation in imagination, dream-making, and a politics of refusal. The sooner you can wrap your hearts and minds around the reality that rest is not a privilege or a luxury but a divine and human right that is always available to us when we reimagine, the richer the beauty of rest will be made plain to you. It will be a slow unraveling, so do not try and take this information in quickly and do not attempt to try and ignore your fear. Take a deep breath and slowly imagine your life well-rested. Give yourself grace and mercy. It is yours to cocoon and swaddle yourself in. You can rest! You can imagine. If it sounds scary or impossible, that is part of the process. You can create a portal of rest, care, and imagination at any time. Resting is our divine right. Our birth anoints us with the power of divinity.

This work is about more than naps and is about more than literal sleep. How do I unravel? How do I deprogram? The answer is you do it slowly. You do it with intention. You do it with care. You do it simply by believing that you deserve to rest. Our self-esteem and self-worth have been wrecked by capitalism, patriarchy, ableism, and racism. All have made us believe we aren't worthy and that we must prove ourselves by pushing hard every day to be able to receive love, care, rest, grace. It cannot be repeated enough how abusive this lie is to us. Grind culture has thrown us into believing that suffering, hyperproductivity, and constant doing is redemptive. This is a lie.

Before I decided to begin to experiment with what rest could do for my physical and spiritual body, I was pushing myself to the limit every day. I was totally unaware that I was doing this because of a lifelong brainwashing at the hands of capitalism and white supremacy. I was simply doing what everyone around me was doing. I was simply trying to pay bills, go to school, take care of my child, and navigate my world in a way that felt like survival. I had no outside perspective on how this machine-level pace was exhausting me. Everyone around me was on this pace. All the demands of my job, classes, friends, and family resided in a cycle of constant labor. Silence and stillness only came when I would finally crawl into the bed after a fifteen-hour day of classes, work, and parenting.

This rest movement is an outlier movement because all the world is in collaboration for us not to rest. Capitalism rages on and we are holding on by a thread to remain outside of extreme poverty. We are trained to be machinelike and to my conscious mind it felt normal. When I began to rest, even a twenty-minute nap or ten minutes of daydreaming daily, the portal of rest opened, and my physical and spiritual body began to cry out for more.

This is a mindset, a paradigm shift, and an ethos that will take time. I looked to my Ancestors for inspiration and maybe you can look to yours for that same inspiration. This work is rooted in community care and the collective, so look for others around you who are curious about healing. Your rested heart will begin to organically connect with other weary souls seeking rest and care. I looked to those who came before me and found ways to hold space for their healing. I looked to those working daily trying to make a way and was inspired.

When I think about a DreamSpace, I think about a sacred place. A well of knowledge. A place we can go to that is unlike the weight of this world. A resting place for us to enter in to work things out. My deepest DreamSpace came to me while I was sleeping on a couch one day. I was watching TV and had an unplanned nap—my favorite kind—and as I went more into this rested state, I began to feel as if my entire body was expanding into the couch. I felt like I was being hugged by softness. I woke up in less than thirty minutes refreshed and ready for the day. I think about a DreamSpace being a place that we really cannot imagine. Our deepest imaginings are waiting for us there: our truest rest, our pathway to healing, the place we go to feel safe. This is what happens when we rest.

There is information in your body that wants to be heard. There is information in your body that will allow you to tap into the innermost parts of yourself. This work is about embodiment. It is not about endlessly talking about rest or creating social media memes about rest. It is not about repeating all the things that our body already knows. Your body has important information to share with you but it can only arrive to you in a rested state. What if you are missing so much of who you are because you are navigating life from a state of exhaustion?

I believe there is so much guidance that can get us into the next dimension of our liberation waiting for us in our rested state, in our dream state, in a slowed-down and quiet state. How much are we missing because we are constantly on the go and busy creating moments to fill calendars? When will we make space for our bodies to reflect and for our hearts to widen so we can connect with who we are? Our exhaustion is leading us down the path of destruction. Our exhaustion will not lead us to liberation. Nothing can come from exhaustion but more exhaustion and more toxicity and terror. The time to rest is now.

How to Imagine

We imagine by being in community. We imagine by receiving and offering radical care. We imagine by embracing and running toward our interconnectedness. Individualism is leading us to the path of exhaustion and death. Community care will save us, and we can dream up all the ways to manifest and strategize the care of communities. One of my most transformational moments of community care and interconnectedness came when my father died suddenly, and I was embraced by community. The witnesses surrounded me and my family's every move. My mama, the new widow after forty years of loving this man, was tended to like a newborn baby. Her eight siblings flew in from all over the country to be her witness and to lament with her. To cook her grits in the morning, to lay in bed with her, to camp out in the basement on couches and floors. If she needed anything, it was there in one second.

This is sacred community. This is the interconnectedness that is key to our liberation. When we stand in the gaps for each other and decide to be relentless in our support and witness, we can shift oppression. The beauty of this reality is that it repeats itself in many forms on our journey in life: at graduations and weddings. In classrooms and courtrooms, on protest marches and elevators, on battlefields and in gang territory, during childbirth and even in death. We are intimately tied to each other. We can find divinity and rest through each other.

Given this experience of seeing the work of interconnectedness in action, how is it related to the liberation of exhausted people in an oppressive, capitalist society? How can those living on the margins activate the power of mutuality for collective healing against grind culture? Can an encounter with community lead persons resisting grind culture to liberation and imagination? How does our collective daydreaming build community? How can we come together to disrupt capitalism via rest?

Dr. Martin Luther King Jr. is one of my paper mentors. In an excerpt from the classic text *Why We Can't Wait,* Dr. King outlines the importance of intentional community building and the power of organizing for liberation. When confronted with the harsh reality of leading a nonviolent protest for civil rights in Birmingham, Alabama, Dr. King created a radical army of volunteers who would help sustain the movement. He explains: "The invitational periods at the mass meetings, when we asked for volunteers, were much like those invitational periods that occur each Sunday morning in Negro churches; the pastor projects the call to those present to join the church. We did not hesitate to call our movement an army. But it was a special army, with no supplies but its sincerity, no uniform but its determination, no arsenal except its faith, no currency but its conscience."[3] This army becomes a connected group of trained individuals committed to a cause and ready to fight spiritually for local change. This is the sacredness of radical community.

Our rest work understands that the current system will not give us rest and we will only be able to experiment with rest as resistance with a trained and conscious community of people. We cannot heal alone, and we must craft our rest practices in a collective way with our North Star being disruption, refusal, and healing. As Dr. King said, "Freedom is never voluntarily given by the oppressor. It must be demanded by the oppressed." Our interconnectedness is a form of resistance in times thriving against the dehumanizing ways capitalism and white supremacy see the world. Those caught up and aligned with either system must do the important work of looking at themselves with an open heart and determined Spirit to change and transform. There is deeper unraveling to be done. Our care and rest will open up a new future story.

We must be determined. Grind culture keeps us out of our imagination and in a constant state of explanation, on the edge of tears, exhausted, triggered, and wondering. How could an interconnected radical embrace of imagination and rest serve as a form of liberation? How can we build a fortress of care and live into our role as neighbor? I believe our very survival spiritually against grind culture resides in community care. We are nothing without each other. We will be nothing, will seek to exist, if we don't look closely at our own trauma around the violence of grind culture. How are you participating as an agent of grind culture? Are you aligning yourself with those who seek to exploit our labor and attention? I want us free from inflicting violence unto ourselves and each other because we haven't stopped long enough or stepped back to analyze what happens when we attempt to keep up with grind culture. There is no way to keep up with the machine-level pace that capitalism requires. It is not sustainable and the first step in moving away from this pace to craft spaces of rest and care is to grow your imagination.

The idea of rest as resistance is a counternarrative to the dominant story. Protest and resistance don't look one way. It's what's really happening on the ground in the small and important details of our lives. It says, "No, this isn't the full story. I have another perspective. I can speak for myself." It's living when someone told you you should die. It's centering joy when pain and oppression surround you daily. It's living in your truth, even when your heart trembles at the thought of being vulnerable. It's napping when the entire culture calls you lazy. It's sleeping when you have been told by capitalism that you aren't doing enough. It's honoring a day, a week, a second for Sabbath. It's reimagining what a Sabbath can look like based on your own history. Resistance is laying down when you have been told to keep going. It's listening to the voice whispering inside of you to be productive when your breathing is all the production ever needed. Just keep resting. Keep repeating to yourself and those around you that rest is your resistance. Repetition is a powerful concept for deprogramming and I hope you stay with your head on a pillow and in the stars imagining new worlds. Repeat the following meditations over and over.

Meditations for rest

1. I deserve to rest now.
2. I am worthy of rest.

3. I am not lazy. How could I be lazy? My Ancestors are too brilliant for that.
4. Capitalism wants my body to be a machine. I am not a machine.
5. I am a magical and divine human being.
6. I have the right to resist grind culture.
7. I don't have to earn rest.
8. Do less, watch how I thrive.
9. Ease is my birthright.
10. I Will Rest!

Conclusion

Go to your beds. Go to your couches. Find a hammock. Go into the portal of naps. Go there often. You don't have to wait on permission from the dominant culture. Your body is divine and sovereign. Go to your spaces of rest, joy, and freedom. Create them in your imagination. Create them in your communities. Create them in your homes. Create them in your workspaces. Create them in your heart. Daydream collectively. Do all these things with others. We will not heal alone. We will not thrive alone. Communal care is our saving grace and our communion. Community care will save us. It is already saving us. There will not be instant answers to our inquiries about rest as resistance. We don't desire anything quick and instant because both ignore our complexities as human beings. We must be more human. We want to bathe and soak in our complexities. We want to take our sweet time. We want to tap into the bottomless well of wisdom and surprise waiting for us inside the portal of rest. There is power in nuance and expansiveness. Go to the water. Go to the depths of the ocean inside of you. Float there. Rest there. Imagine and dream there. It is game over for the lies of white supremacy and capitalism. We know better. The veils have been lifted and with each nap we are closer to seeing ourselves for who we truly are. We know this will not be easy as the systems will most likely gain more power before they ultimately burn themselves out. As we collectively rest and unravel from our alignment with grind culture, layers are peeled back to show the truth of ourselves. We are more than what we have ever been told and we must continue seeing each other and ourselves, no matter how distorted and exhausted we show up. Take to your beds. Accept all you have ignored and then rest more. What does your body want? What does your soul need? What are the whispers that have been silenced by the cranking gears of grind culture? What have we missed in our urgency and rushing? This is just the beginning and for this truth we must be grateful for the awareness, the information, and the reclaimed power and time. This is a transmission. A manifesto for the rest pilgrimage. Come back to it often. Keep it close. The message will keep repeating. View it as evidence that you are not alone in your desire to be liberated from exhaustion. Our battle cry and mantra: "WE WILL REST!" Say it in your hearts, whisper it aloud, repeat it as you fall asleep, tell your neighbor, "We will rest! We will rest! We will rest!"

ACKNOWLEDGMENTS

This book would not exist without the following people lifting me up and wrapping me in the purest community care energy. Deep gratitude to:

My husband and partner in life Tommy. When I wanted to quit, you wouldn't allow it. Your words, presence and forever support have made my time creating this book soft and protected.

Helen Hale, my art collaborator, and creative sister. The art we have created with prayers, candles and vision has been life-shifting. Thank you for being in the underworld of possibility with me.

My deepest gratitude to my community in Atlanta and in my hometown of Chicago that believed in this rest message from the moment I uttered a whisper about it. The ones who have volunteered hours of their time to curate sacred spaces for rest and care:

Yellow Mat Wellness, John and Katherine Heinz, Free

Street Theater in Chicago, Krista Franklin, Jamila Raegan, Tracie Hall of Rootwork Gallery, Charlie Watts, The Black Mecca Project and most importantly the thousands of people who have come to our rest installations to nap and hold space for community care. Thank you for trusting me to guide you into the portal of rest, for your vulnerability and commitment to disrupting. May we all find and create moments of rest wherever we are.

BIBLIOGRAPHY

THE NAP MINISTRY LIBRARY

These books have been a quiet storm in my understanding of liberation, rest, and resistance. May they be a collaborator for your lifelong rest pilgrimage. It may take years to truly engage with just one title from this list. Please don't rush or see this as a reading competition. There is no urgency, only the joy of lifelong rest, study, and research.

Why We Can't Wait Martin Luther King, Jr.

A Black Theology of Liberation James Cone

Womanist Theological Ethics: A Reader edited by Katie Geneva Cannon, Emilie M. Townes, and Angela D. Sims

Renaissance Ruth Forman

Slave Testimony: Two Centuries of Letters, Speeches, Interviews, and Autobiographies edited by John. W. Blassingame

Slavery's Exiles: The Story of the American Maroons Sylviane A. Diouf

Bibliography

Making a Way Out of No Way: A Womanist Theology Monica A. Coleman

Parable of the Sower Octavia Butler

All About Love: New Visions bell hooks

The Selected Works of Audre Lorde Audre Lorde, edited by Roxane Gay

Meditations from the Heart Howard Thurman

NOTES

INTRODUCTION

1. Blassingame, James W. *Slave Testimony: Two Centuries of Letters, Speeches, Interviews, and Autobiographies*, Baton Rouge and London: Louisiana State University Press, 1977. Pages 217, 218.

PART ONE

1. Sandoiu, Ana, "Do Black Americans get less sleep than white Americans?," Medical News Today, August 18, 2020.
2. Walker, Alice, *In Search of Our Mothers' Gardens*, New York: Mariner Books, 2003.
3. Coleman, Monica A., *Making a Way Out of No Way: A Womanist Theology*, Minneapolis: Fortress Press, 2008. Page 86.
4. Thompson, Derek, "Social Media Is Attention Alcohol," *The Atlantic*, September 17, 2021.
5. Cone, James H., *A Black Theology of Liberation: Fortieth Anniversary Edition*, New York: Orbis Books, 2010. Page 27.
6. hooks, bell, *all about love: New Visions*, New York: HarperCollins, 2001.

PART TWO

1. Butler, Octavia, *Parable of the Sower*, New York: Four Walls Eight Windows, 1993.

2. Cannon, Katie Geneva, Emilie M. Townes, and Angela D. Sims, *Womanist Theological Ethics: A Reader*, Louisville: Westminster John Knox Press, 2011.
3. Lorde, Audre, *The Selected Works of Audre Lorde*, New York: W. W. Norton, 2020.
4. Blassingame, James W., *Slave Testimony: Two Centuries of Letters, Speeches, Interviews, and Autobiographies*, Baton Rouge and London: Louisiana State University Press, 1977. Pages 109, 217, 218, 220, 221.
5. hooks, bell, "Love as the Practice of Freedom," in *Outlaw Culture: Resisting Representations*, New York: Routledge Classics, 1994.

PART THREE

1. Diouf, Sylviane A., *Slavery's Exiles: The Story of the American Maroons*, New York: New York University Press, 2014.
2. Ibid., page 380.

PART FOUR

1. Butler, Octavia, "A Few Rules for Predicting the Future," *Essence*, 2000.
2. Hsu, Hua, "How Sun Ra Taught Us to Believe in the Impossible," *The New Yorker*, June 28, 2021.
3. King Jr., Martin Luther, "Letter from Birmingham Jail," April 16, 1963.

INDEX

ableism, 119, 185
academia, grind culture in, 25, 79–80, 115–117
accessibility
  of imagination/invention, 148
  of rest, 63–66
accomplishments
  dedicating every moment to, 80
  worth based on, 117, 162
accountability, spaces for, 106
action, practical, 160
active rest, 120
activism
  collective rest as form of, 67
  resurrection for, 182–183
addiction, to social media, 67–72, 165, 166
Afrofuturism, 175–179
all about love (hooks), 77
American maroons, 133–135, 141–142
Ancestors, inspiration from, 36, 186–187
anti-Blackness, 119
approval, to rest, 72–73
artists, 32–33, 125
Atlanta, Ga., 175
attention, turning, away from trauma, 140

baths, 151
being, new ways of, 97
binary systems, 96, 125
Black Church, 47–48, 74, 181–182
Black excellence, 80
Black history, 73–74
Black liberation. *See also* liberation
  to benefit all of humanity, 75–77
  resistance for, 131–132
  womanism and, 57
Black Liberation theology, 73–75
Black Panther (film), 176
Black people
  burden of labor for Black women, 62–63, 168–169
  capitalism connected to, 73
  in Rest as Resistance movement, 78
  rest for, 103–104
  sleep gap for, 54
Black Theology of Liberation (Cone), 73–74
Blackness, 78
body(-ies)
  as agent for change, 12
  connecting mind and, 120, 138–140
  destruction of, 32
  knowledge within, 173, 187–188
  rested, 139
  restoring your, 78–79
  as tools for oppression, 133
  transformation for, 167
boundaries, between work and labor, 167

Index

brain love, 93. *See also* daydreaming
brainwashed people. *See also* deprogramming from brainwashing
  exhaustion for, 15
  grind culture's impact on, 20
  in public school systems, 23–24
  rest for, 23–24, 60, 170
  waking up, 29, 98
breathing exercises, 138
busyness, 21, 87
Butler, Octavia, 95, 159–160, 170, 176

call to work harder, 47
calm, moments of, 31
capitalism
  aligning with, 172
  binary systems in, 125
  Black liberation to disrupt, 75–77
  busyness in, 21
  deconstructing, 122
  dreaming to disrupt, 97, 113, 125, 179
  as form of plantation labor, 15, 38
  in grind culture, 12, 38, 83
  healing and liberation from, 33
  Willie Hersey's lessons on, 49
  imagination to disrupt, 169–170, 186, 191
  impact of, on Earth, 163–164
  impact of, on rest, 54, 61, 161, 164–165
  invention and, 179
  machine-level labor in, 20, 96–97, 124
  productivity in, 21, 62
  resistance to disrupt, 142–143, 154–155
  rest to disrupt, 13–19, 29
  scarcity in, 16
  self-esteem, self-worth, and, 185
  social media as extension of, 27–28, 71–72, 169
  white supremacy and, 35

care
  community, 120, 164, 188–189, 191
  creating systems of, 141
  power from, 82
  treating yourself with, 61
Caston, Ora, 5–6, 14, 43, 48, 104–105, 180
catnaps, 137
Chicago, Ill., 46–47
chronic disease, 51–52
Civil Rights Movement, 35, 46–47, 104
clarity, about what rest is, 55–56
Coleman, Monica, 58, 59
collective dreaming, 106
Collective Napping Experience, 64–65
  for dreaming, 107–113
  invocation of, 40–41, 110–111
collective rest
  to change the world, 12
  and DreamSpace, 11–12
  as form of activism, 67
  and interconnectedness, 78
  liberation from, 7–8
  to save ourselves, 105
colonized, being, 16–17
community
  cultivating, 106
  support from, 107
community care, 164, 188–189, 191
community resurrection, 182–183
Cone, James, 73–75
connection. *See* disconnection; interconnectedness
control, myth of, 140
convenience-style processing, 173
corporations, 161
cup metaphor, for rest, 62–63
curiosity, for resistance, 149–150
cycle of trauma, 81, 106

daydreaming. *See also* dreaming
  benefits of, 105
  as brain love, 93–94
  forgetting factors for, 99–100

and "let the chips fall where they may" approach, 102–103
poetry as form of, 100–103
as resistance, 132
decolonization, 25–26, 62
deprogramming from brainwashing
Afrofuturism for, 177–179
DreamSpace for, 98
freedom from, 123–125
of minds and hearts, 150
repetition and meditation for, 192–193
as resistance, 136–137
rest for, 62
Diouf, Sylviane A., 135
disconnection
busyness and exhaustion as cause of, 87
capitalism as cause of, 15
grind culture as cause of, 96
imagination and, 164
inner knowing replaced by, 55
disruption, 182–183
divinity, connecting to and reclaiming your, 62
dream lessons, 95
dreaming, 91, 93–126
benefits of, 105
for Black people, 103–104
as a collective, 105–106, 118–119
and Collective Napping Experience, 107–113
to connect mind and body, 120–121
for deprogramming, 123–125, 165–166
to disrupt capitalism, 125–126
to disrupt exhaustion, 103, 121–122
embracing ability for, 114–117
ideas to inspire, 151–152
liberation from, 98–99, 113
love for, 118–119, 120
and misconceptions about rest, 122–123
questions to prepare for, 162–163
and Resurrect Rest School, 118–119
as space for resistance, 142
techniques for, 106–107
DreamSpace
Afrofuturism inspiring, 177
collective rest and, 11–12
deprogramming with, 165–166
to disrupt capitalism, 97
imagination and, 187
learning and unlearning to visit, 119
practice and vision for, 106
reclaiming, 13, 34–38
tapping into, 181
theft of, 160

efficiency, 23
Elliott, Missy, 176
emotional labor, exploitation of, 169
energy, of refusal, 132
escape artists, 125
escapism, 171
Essence (Butler), 170
"Ethics as an Art of Doing the Work Our Souls Must Have" (Townes), 98
exhaustion
consequences of, 121
culture of, 12
daydreaming to reduce, 103
Earth's state of, 163–164
joy and connections stolen by, 87
legacy of, 17–18
liberation and, 188
productivity and, 150
socialization of, 15
existing, simply, 80
expanding, to nap, 151
experimentation
grind culture's theft of, 87–88
for resistance, 149–150

faith, radical, 103, 142
fear
in grind culture, 86, 137
socialization of, 20–22

Index

"A Few Rules for Predicting the Future" (Butler), 170
freedom
  liberation vs., 98
  to manage your deprogramming journey, 123–125
  resistance for, 153

Giovanni, Nikki, 175
Girl Trek organization, 109–110
giving, mutual, 77–78
Great Migration, 6, 46
grieving, 15, 19, 28
grind culture
  in academia, 25, 79–80, 115–117
  Afrofuturism to deprogram from, 177–179
  being agents of, 23–24
  being outliers and risk takers in, 166–167
  bodies ignored in, 182
  capitalism and white supremacy in, 12, 38, 83
  community impacted by, 87
  cycle of trauma in, 81, 106
  deprogramming from, 15–17, 177–179
  destruction of bodies in, 32
  and doing more of the same, 66
  dreaming to disrupt, 125–126, 165–16
  fear in, 20–22, 86, 137
  impact of, on dreaming, 99–100
  impact of, on humanity, 76
  impact of, on imagination, 191
  and knowledge about rest, 60
  pace of, 96
  participation in, 17
  physical and spiritual destruction caused by, 54
  pleasure, hobbies, leisure, and experimentation stolen by, 87–88
  in public school systems, 22–23
  refusal of, 11
  resisting, 135–137, 153
  scarcity in, 86
  silence and rested bodies to disrupt, 139
  social media as tool for, 70
  "successful," 24
  toxic sayings promoting, 86
  urgency in, 20–22
  violence in, 113, 150
guilt, rest and, 113–114

Hamer, Fannie Lou, 77
healing
  imagination as factor in, 173
  naps as portal to, 13, 26–34
  resistance as factor in, 153
  rest as factor in, 33
hearts, deprogramming, 150
Hersey, Willie, 47, 49–53, 79–81, 188–189
history, dreaming to process, 94
hobbies, 87–88
hooks, bell, 77, 119, 120, 157, 159–160
hope, 170–171
Hughes, Langston, 175
humanity, 50, 75–77
hustling to survive, 15, 88, 153
hyperproductivity, 23, 67

imagination, 157, 159–195
  accessibility of, 148
  Afrofuturism to inspire, 175–179
  being firmly planted in, 174
  and being realistic, 183–184
  to discover possibilities, 171–172
  to disrupt capitalism, 169–170, 186, 191
  and DreamSpace, 187
  examples of, 188–189
  exhaustion's impact on, 121
  hope inspired by, 170–171
  to identify rest, 161
  and interconnectedness, 189–191

and knowledge within bodies and souls, 173, 187–188
for liberation, 159–161, 188
for The Nap Ministry, 174
naps as portal to, 13, 26–34
oppression's theft of, 183
and poetry, 175
and proving your worth, 162
resistance and, 179–180, 183, 192
rest to make space for, 161–162
resurrection and, 182–183
Sabbath to encourage, 163–167
science fiction to inspire, 176–179
underestimating, 171
In Search of Our Mother's Gardens (Walker), 56
individualism, 18, 120, 188
inherent worth, 87
inner knowing, 55
inspiration, from ancestors, 186–187
intention, 185
interconnectedness
and collective rest, 78
and connectedness, 166
imagination and, 189–191
resistance and, 76–77
intimacy, 106, 113
intuition, 121, 166
invention
accessibility of, 148
naps as portal to, 13, 26–34
rest for, 160–163

Jefferson, Madison, 36
Jim Crow terrorism, 4, 5, 46, 125, 180
joy, busyness and exhaustion stealing, 87

King, Martin Luther, Jr., 77, 104, 190
knowledge
about how to rest, 60
within bodies and souls, 173, 187–188

labor
Black women's burden of, 62–63, 168–169
boundaries between work and, 167
exploitation of, 169
Latino women's burden of, 63
machine-level, 20, 96–97, 124
marginalized women and, 62–63
productivity and increased, 94
profits from increased, 95
social media as form of, 169
Latino women, burden of labor for, 63
learning
ability to learn new ways of being, 97
to visit DreamSpace, 119
leisure, grind culture's theft of, 87–88
"let the chips fall where they may" approach, 102–103
liberation
Afrofuturism as an example of, 177
bodies as site of, 13, 19–26, 149
and exhaustion, 188
freedom vs., 98
grieving as place of, 28
and imagination, 159–161, 188
interconnectedness for, 189
as lifelong practice, 98–99
rest for, 25–26, 33, 73, 165
listening, 139
Lorde, Audre, 61, 100
love
community care and, 118–119
rest as form of, 147–148
"Love as a Practice of Freedom" (hooks), 119
luxury, rest as, 28–29, 152

machine-level labor, 20, 96–97, 124
Making a Way Out of No Way (Coleman), 58
maroons, 133–135, 141–142
Mason, Charles H., 47
McMillian, Harry, 145–146

meditation practices, 34, 162–163, 192–193
memory, imagination and, 180
mercy, 167
metaphysical world, dreams and, 96
Metaverse, 70
mind(s)
connecting body and, 120, 138–140
deprogramming, 150
rest to restore, 78–79
moments to be human, 50
money, worth attached to, 19–20
motivation, dreams to find, 97
mutual giving, 77–78
mutual rest, 78. *See also* collective rest

Nap Bishop, 75, 111
The Nap Ministry, 13–38
Ancestors as inspiration for, 36
availability of rest and, 63
and being an escape artist, 125
Black Liberation theology and, 73, 75
bodies as site of liberation, 13, 19–26
Collective Napping Experience at, 64–65, 107–113
for disruption of capitalism and white supremacy, 13, 14–19
grieving as factor in, 19
history as foundation of, 104
imagination as factor in, 170, 174
invocation of, 40–41, 110–111
library of, 199–200
meditation in, 33
naps as portal to imagine, invent, and heal, 13, 26–34
reclaiming of DreamSpace, 13, 34–38
resistance as factor in, 132–133, 146
Rest is Resistance framework and, 26, 39
Slave Testimony's impact on, 114–115
starting, 4–5
tenets of, 13–38
and ways to rest, 85–86
Nap Talk sessions, 108, 110
naps
catnaps, 137
to deprogram mind, 150
dream and vision space during, 143
as portal to imagine, invent, and heal, 13, 26–34
and upholding oppressive systems, 119–120
Newsom, Carol, 127
normalcy, of machine pace, 96–97
"Not-To-Do Lists," 83

one-time event, resting as, 62, 63
opportunities to rest, 72–73, 149
oppression
bodies as tools for, 133
history of, 35
imagination stolen by, 176, 183
outdoors, getting, 30
outliers, 166–167

pace, of grind culture, 96
Parable of the Sower (Butler), 95
Parks, Rosa, 104
patience, 167
patriarchy
amd women's burden of labor, 62
love and care vs., 119
self-esteem / self-worth and, 185
womanism to disrupt, 57
peace, moments of, 31
perfectionism, 117
physical destruction, grind culture as cause of, 54
physical labor, exploitation of, 169
plantation labor
capitalism as form of, 15, 38
Madison Jefferson's testimony about, 36–37
pleasure, grind culture's theft of, 87–88
poetry, 100–103, 151, 175
"Poetry Is Not a Luxury" (Lorde), 100

possibilities, imagination to discover, 171–172
poverty, 161
power
from rest, 88
of the tongue, 124
transmuting trauma to, 182
practice, 84–86, 106
privilege, rest as, 152, 184–185
productivity
capitalism as cult of, 21
constant state of, 62
exhaustion from, 150
increased labor and, 94
timelines geared for, 125
worth and, 19–20
protests, 192
public school systems, 22–23

racism, 185. *See also* white supremacy
radical faith, 103, 142
rage, 79
realistic, being, 183–184
refusal, energy of, 132
reparation, rest as, 26, 27, 73
repetition, 192–193
resistance, 127, 129–155
for Black liberation, 131–132
connecting mind and body as, 138–140
curiosity and experimentation for, 149–150
and daydreaming, 132
to disrupt capitalism, 153
to disrupt grind culture, 135–137, 140–141
to disrupt white supremacy, 147
dream and vision spaces for, 142
foundation of, 78, 142–143
history of, 133–135
ideas to facilitate, 151–152
and imagination, 154, 179–180, 183, 192
and interconnectedness, 76–77
myths about, 152
naps as form of, 27, 151–152
reclaiming autonomy and leisure as, 141–142
rest as part of, 35, 147–148
to slavery, 133–135, 144–146
soul as driver of, 129–131
rest, 43, 45–89. *See also* collective rest
academia's impact on, 79–80
accessibility of, 63–66
active, 120
as battle for liberation, 165
Black Liberation theology for, 73–76
call to action for, 45
clarity about, 55–56
in Collective Napping Experience, 64–66
consequences of refusing to, 45–55
cup metaphor about, 62–63
to disrupt grind culture, 66–67, 86–88
factors impacting ability to, 61–63
finding space to, 59–60
grind culture's impact on, 60
guilt and shame about, 113–114
to heal bodies and minds, 78–79
and interconnectedness, 76–78
as luxury, 28–29, 152
meditation practice for, 34
misconceptions about, 122–123
model for, 60
mutual, 78
as one-time event, 62, 63
opportunities to, 72–73, 149
as part of living, 35
people who would benefit from, 82–83
permission to, 72–73
plans to, 30
as privilege, 152, 184–185
as reparation, 26, 27, 73
as resistance, 78, 81
and slowing down, 85, 106

rest *(cont.)*
social media's impact on, 67–72
as spiritual practice, 18
talking and writing about, 165
ways to, 81–86, 142–143
womanism and, 56–58
Rest Is Resistance framework. *See also specific actions in*
Afrofuturism as factor in, 177
and Black Liberation theology, 73
to disrupt capitalism, 62
institutions and governments in, 172
and The Nap Ministry, 39
to provide availability of rest, 63
resistance as factor in, 81
and Resurrect Rest School, 118–119
rest meditation practice, 34
rested futures, 179, 183
restoration, 161–162
Resurrect Rest School, 118–119
resurrection, community, 182–183
reverence, 28
revolution, 173
rigidity, in white supremacy, 96
risk takers, 31–32, 166–167
Robbins Church of God in Christ (C.O.G.I.C.), 47

Sabbath, 163–167
scarcity, 16, 86
self-esteem, 185
self-worth, 185
sexism, 57, 62
shame, rest and, 113–114
side hustles, 88
silence
to disrupt grind culture, 139
and dreams, 151
as form of rest, 68–69
poetry as a place of, 101
sky gazing, 137
Slave Testimony (anthology), 36, 114–115, 144
slavery
Madison Jefferson's testimony about, 36–37
resistance to, 133–135, 144–146
Slavery's Exiles (Diouf), 135
sleep deprivation
chronic disease and, 51–52
grind culture as cause of, 12, 15
as public health issue, 18, 54
as racial issue, 33
as social justice issue, 33, 54
sleep gap, for Black Americans, 54
slowing down
creating space to dream by, 106
to disrupt grind culture, 82–83
to reimagine rest, 85
as rest, 106
social media
addictive qualities of, 67–72, 165, 166
detoxing from, 30, 68–69, 71–72, 151, 183
DreamSpace impacted by, 34–35
as extension of capitalism, 27–28, 71–72, 183
as form of labor, 169
rest impacted by, 67–72
as tool for grind culture, 70
softness, 151
somatics training, 137
soul(s)
knowledge within, 173, 187–188
transformation of, 167
space
to dream, 106–107
for intimacy, accountability, and vulnerability, 106–107
to rest, 59–66, 149
spiritual destruction, 54
spiritual labor, exploitation of, 169
spiritual practice, rest as, 18
spiritual world, dreams attached to, 96
Star Wars (film series), 176
strength, 88, 180

stress, chronic disease and, 51–52
Stress Protest retreat, 109–110
stretching, 151
subversive, being, 106
Sun Ra, 176–178
surrendering, 139
survival
  hustling for, 15, 88, 153
  thriving vs., 24

tenderness, power from, 82
thriving
  dreaming and, 107
  surviving vs., 24
  and treating yourself with care, 61
Thurman, Howard, 127
Townes, Emilie, 98
trauma
  cycle of, 81, 106
  power from, 182
  responses related to, 81
  turning attention away from, 140
Tubman, Harriet, 132, 183

Underground Railroad, 106, 125, 132
Union Pacific Railroad, 47
unlearning, to visit DreamSpace, 119
urgency
  lie of, 25, 100
  socialization of, 20–22

violence
  in grind culture, 113, 150, 166
  resistance to disrupt systems of, 133–134
virtual experiences, 70–71
vision spaces, 106, 142
vulnerability, 106, 113

wages, low, 161
waking people up
  from being brainwashed, 29, 98
  at Collective Napping Experiences, 112
Walker, Alice, 56, 175
Wall Street Journal, 68
wandering, 106
white supremacy
  aligning with, 172
  as basis for capitalism, 35
  Black liberation to disrupt, 75–77
  deconstructing, 122
  disrupting, 13–19
  in grind culture, 12, 38, 83
  healing and liberation from, 33
  Willie Hersey's lessons on, 49
  impact of, on dreaming/invention, 179
  as opposite of love and care, 119
  perfectionism in, 117
  resistance to disrupt, 155
  rest to disrupt, 29
  rigidity in, 96
Why We Cannot Wait (King Jr.), 190
womanism, 56–58
Womanist Theological Ethics (Townes), 98
work. *See also* labor
  boundaries between labor and, 167
  call to, 47
worth
  accomplishments as basis for, 117, 162
  determining your, 87, 148–149
  productivity/money attached to, 19–20
  rest and, 149
writing, about rest, 165

X, Malcolm, 104

Yellow Mat Yoga and Wellness, 111–112

ABOUT THE AUTHOR

Tricia Hersey is an artist, poet, theologian, and community organizer. She is the founder of The Nap Ministry, an organization that examines rest as a form of resistance by curating sacred spaces for the community to rest via Collective Napping Experiences, immersive workshops, performance art installations, and social media. Tricia is a global pioneer and originator of the movement to understand the liberatory power of rest. She is the creator of the Rest Is Resistance and Rest as Reparations frameworks. Her research interests include Black Liberation theology, womanism, somatics, and cultural trauma. Tricia is a Chicago native and currently lives in southern Georgia.